FROM MANY LANDS

Alberta Eiseman

FROM MANY LANDS

Atheneum 1974 New York

To My Parents

Acknowledgments

We wish to acknowledge material drawn from the following sources:

The American Folklore Society, Inc.: *Folklore in America* edited by Tristram P. Coffin and Mennig Cohen. Copyright © 1966 by Tristram P. Coffin and Mennig Cohen. Reprinted by permission of the American Folklore Society.

Bantam Books, Inc.: "Ot Azoy Neyt a Shnayder (Weary Days Are a Tailor's)" and "Schlof Mayn Kind (Sleep, My Child)" translated by John Anthony Scott. From *The Ballad of America* by John Anthony Scott. Copyright © 1966 by Bantam Books, Inc. All rights reserved.

Harper and Row, Inc.: From p. 93 of *The Rise of David Levinsky* by Abraham Cahan. (Harper & Row, 1917). From p. 179 of *A Nation of Immigrants* by Louis Adamic. (Harper & Row, 1945). Both selections reprinted by permission of Harper & Row, Publishers.

Hill & Wang, Inc.: *How the Other Half Lives* by Jacob A. Riis. Copyright © 1957 by Hill & Wang, Inc. Reprinted with permission of Hill & Wang, Inc.

Houghton Mifflin Co.: *Promised Land* by Mary Antin. Copyright 1911 and 1912 by The Atlantic Monthly Co. Copyright 1912 by Houghton Mifflin Co. Reprinted by permission of Houghton Mifflin Co.

McGraw-Hill Book Company: *Immigrant Saint* by Pietro Di Donato. Copyright © 1960 by Pietro Di Donato. Used with permission of McGraw-Hill Book Company.

McIntosh and Otis, Inc.: *The Coming of the Green* by Leonard Wibberley. Copyright © 1960 by Leonard Wibberley. Reprinted with permission of McIntosh and Otis, Inc.

W. W. Norton & Co.: *America's Concentration Camps* by Allan R. Bosworth. Copyright © 1967 by Allan R. Bosworth. Reprinted with permission of W. W. Norton & Co.

Charles Scribner's Sons: *The Autobiography of Carl Schurz* edited

Contents

FROM MANY LANDS

Prologue

THE YEAR WAS 1907, a raw day in early spring. In the busy harbor of New York, a ferryboat left the side of the steamship *Estonia* and turned toward Ellis Island.

Hundreds of people crowded the decks of the ferry; all of them newcomers to the United States. They wore the costumes of many lands; the fur hats, the flowered kerchiefs, the embroidered petticoats, the high boots, the black shawls of their native villages.

There were some who pointed excitedly at the sights around them, but mostly they huddled silently against one another, frightened and exhausted.

A young boy stood in the crowd, his eyes bright with wonder. He saw the steamships, the squat tugboats that led them into port, the stately buildings of Manhattan in the distance, the giant lady with a torch they called the Statue of Liberty.

He turned to his mother, eager to share his impressions of the new land, but her look was somber, anxious, and he held back his words. In one arm she cradled the baby, the other arm was wrapped tightly around the shoulders of her little daughter. Her eyes, ringed with dark circles, darted nervously about.

In tones of reproach, she reminded him that he was supposed to carry their luggage, not leave it on the floor where it might be stolen.

Jacob did as he was told. He understood his mother's nervousness only too well. He was as tired, as bewildered as she, after the endless journey.

The ferry was approaching the red brick buildings of Ellis Island. Jacob could see a group of uniformed men awaiting them on the dock. The boat stopped with a shudder, and right away the passengers began to push toward the gate. A hum of excited conversation arose, a hum made up of a dozen different tongues.

Jacob tried to stay close to his family. As he stepped off the ferry someone jostled him, and he staggered under the weight of their wicker suitcase, the pillows, the feather bed. A stranger took the suitcase from his hand, murmuring words in a language the boy could not understand. Then the man stood alongside him on the pier, smiling, and Jacob said, slowly and self-consciously, "tank you." The man nodded.

One thing, at least, was no longer frightening, Jacob thought with relief. The babble of unfamiliar tongues had lost its terror after seventeen days of living together in the steerage section of the *Estonia*. There had been so much that was truly frightening on that voyage!

For seventeen days the ship had heaved and rocked in the stormy sea. Their quarters, dark and overcrowded, had been a nightmare. Almost three hundred people had lived together in one large room, like cattle in an ill-kept barn.

There they had slept—when sleep would come—one family to a bunk, each bunk no wider than two feet. Between themselves and the top berth, they had had less than three feet of head room. There they had eaten, at one long table stretched along the passageway: bread, herring and potatoes, day after stormy day.

The herring made one thirsty, but water was scarce. Anyway, after the first few days at sea, one could hardly bear to drink it: it tasted foul. Jacob could still smell the herring: it was only one of many acrid odors pervading the steerage area.

For a breath of air and some exercise they had been allowed to go on deck at certain hours of the day. The space reserved for them had been the worst part of the ship, where the motion of the sea was most violent, and the dirt from the smokestacks the worst. Seasickness had been with them always, and dirt, and disease, and human misery.

Jacob shuddered at the memory. Thank heaven that part of the journey was over! He looked up as the uniformed men on the dock shouted some orders at them. The immigrants picked up their baggage and followed in a ragged file.

Once inside the large brick buildings, the new arrivals were arranged in lines, long lines divided by iron railings. At the head of each line a man in uniform sat before a cluttered desk, asking questions of each immigrant.

To those waiting, the words of the interview were undistinguishable, but the tone of the questioner was harsh, the face ever unsmiling. Every so often, after a few moments at the desk, one of the newcomers would be taken aside, a colored tag affixed to his clothing, and he would be walked away, up some metal stairs, out of sight.

Jacob and his mother turned to look at each other. This, then, was the moment father had described in his letters. There would be questions asked, he had warned. Many questions. Watch how you answer them. Be sure you tell the officials that you have relatives in this country, that you will be cared for, that you have some money.

But not much money, Jacob worried as the line inched forward. There was little left of what father had sent. The journey from their village to the seaport had cost more than they had expected. And they still had to buy their tickets to Chicago.

Ah, Chicago! Jacob sighed such a deep sigh that people ahead of him turned to stare. Father and the two older boys would be there to meet them in Chicago. Then, at last, he could go back to being the youngest son in the family!

It was a proud thing to be man of the house, to care for his mother and the two little ones. But a hard thing, too. He had been barely twelve when father left for America, and the baby only a few weeks old. It was more than a year before their steamship tickets arrived. There had been so much to worry about during that year! What if father could not send for them: That had happened to one of his friends. What if they were chased from their village? Where would they go?

The baby coughed, and mother quickly put a hand on her mouth so no one would hear. That frightened the baby, and she started to cry. Jacob smiled at her, gave her his hand to play with. The crying stopped. Mother gave him a grateful look.

What would happen if the inspector found one of them ill, Jacob wondered. Would they have to stay on the island? Would they be turned back? To take that voyage again was too dreadful to consider.

They moved slowly forward. Jacob counted twenty lines. He amused himself by trying to guess the nationalities of the people waiting. After a time they could clearly hear the inspector at the head of their line. Another man stood by his side, translating. That was fortunate! Jacob had a little notebook in his pocket in which he had written each new word of English that he had learned. Still, the booklet held no more than two dozen words; hardly enough to answer all the questions they would be asked.

"It is our turn," mother whispered to him finally, and the long wait was over.

They stood before the uniformed official. He looked up from a long sheet of paper on his desk, fixed a cold stare on Jacob, his mother and the two little girls. Beside him stood the interpreter, dapper and smooth shaven. He speaks our language, Jacob thought, yet he certainly looks foreign!

The questions began to come, directed first at Jacob's mother.

"Your name?"

Voice shaking, she replied.

"Age? Marital status? What age are your children?"

Each question had been asked before they embarked. At each reply, the inspector looked at the list on his desk—the ship's manifest—to make sure the answers checked.

"Where were you born?" the inspector wanted to know, and the interpreter translated. "Who paid for your passage? Where is your husband now? Is he here to meet you?"

Oh, I wish he were, thought Jacob. I wish someone were! He knew, of course, that they would have to wait until they reached Chicago before seeing a familiar face. There was not enough money for someone to come and greet them in New York.

It had taken father over a year to save enough for their passage from Europe. And before that, Jacob's older brothers had worked many long months so they could send for father. Now the family would finally be together.

Father had written that there was a job waiting for Jacob in the clothing factory where he worked. He would have to make believe he was sixteen, but that was easy. Luckily, he was pretty tall. But how did one work in a language one did not understand? And would there still be time for school?

The inspector turned to Jacob and started to question him. The man's voice was bored and cold, and Jacob found himself thinking that he sounded much like the uniformed men back home.

"How much schooling have you had?" the inspector

asked. "Can you read and write?"

To that the boy could answer with pride, because he had been considered a fine student in the village. The official, however, was not impressed. He nodded to the doctor who had joined them. The doctor thumped Jacob's chest, looked closely at his eyes, made him open his mouth and say "ah."

But they did all this before we left Europe, Jacob thought wearily. Still, he supposed they could have caught some illness on the ship. Many, many passengers had. He remembered the morning he had awakened to find that one of the children in a nearby bunk had died during the night.

The doctor began to examine Jacob's sister. Terrified, she clung to her mother's shawl and refused to let him touch her.

"What's the matter with her?" the doctor asked. "Is she dumb? Or deaf?"

Mother bristled. "She is frightened, Your Excellency. She is not used to speaking with strangers."

"Tell the gentleman your name," Jacob whispered to her. "He will not hurt you."

Shyly, the little girl let go of her mother, told the men her name and age.

The inspector waved a hand, finally satisfied.

A tag was affixed to their clothes, and they were pushed ahead, toward a wooden partition. Did that mean they were finished?

Another immigrant took their place before the desk.

Many people were waiting on the other side of the wooden barrier.

Americans, Jacob thought. They are Americans!

The boy and his mother looked around, bewildered, wondering what would happen next. Somehow they had to find some food, buy tickets to Chicago, get on a train.

If only one of those expectant-looking people were there for them!

A lady in a long black skirt and a fine white shirt stepped up to them, speaking their language. She was not dressed like them, yet her smile was warm, and she was offering help.

"Do you need any assistance?" the lady inquired. "Do you have a place to go, or are you being met?"

They told her they had to buy train tickets, showed her what little money they had left. She showed them where to exchange it for dollars, and went with them to make sure they were not cheated. She told them how to take the ferry to the shore, explained where they would find the railroad station.

Finally she handed each of them a package of food and wished them good luck in their new life.

At last they found the station. A man came up to them, wanting to carry their luggage. Jacob stared at him in amazement. His skin was darker than any he had ever seen, darker even than a farmer's face at the end of a long summer. The boy started to hand him their suitcase, for his arms were sore with so much carrying, but mother shook her head fearfully.

They found an empty bench in the waiting room and opened their food packages.

There was meat, and a sweet with berries in it, and a fruit, crescent-shaped, yellow, with brown spots on the skin, such as none of them had ever seen. The only thing missing was bread.

"With just some bread," mother said, looking at last a little happier, "we can make this last until we meet father."

"I will go and buy some bread for us," Jacob said, trying to appear confident. "Wait for me right here."

He found his way out of the station. After walking a few moments he came to a small store and went in, clutching a dollar tightly in his hand.

A tall man stood behind the counter, and addressed him in rapid English.

Jacob felt his courage give way. He took from his pocket

the dictionary his teacher had given him as a farewell present. He looked up "bread," then he looked up "give."

He thought his voice would never come up from his throat.

"Give," he said faintly. Then he pointed to himself. Then "Bread." The second word came out a shout.

"Give bread," he repeated, more evenly.

The man smiled, nodded and reached above the counter.

Jacob put the dollar in his hand. The man gave him back many coins, and handed him the bread.

Jacob walked out of the store, the long loaf tucked securely under his arm.

"He understood me," he said to himself in amazement. "He understood my English. The man in the store understood me."

The words formed a sing-song in his mind, and he walked a little faster. He slipped the change into his pocket, felt the dictionary and gave it a grateful pat.

Then he strode into the station, head held high.

A Nation of Immigrants

S O STARTED THE AMERICAN EXPERIENCE of a
young man coming to a new country. It was a scene that
was to be repeated more than a million times during that
single year of 1907.

Jacob and the others who landed on a spring day at the
start of this century were part of one of the most stirring episodes in the history of the United States: the era of mass immigration.

Immigration itself—the coming of new people into a new
land—had begun shortly after the historic voyage of Christopher Columbus in 1492. He and the explorers who followed
left behind members of their expeditions in isolated settlements on the new continent.

On landing, the voyagers from Europe encountered varied tribes of people they called "Indians." Most of them at
first welcomed the settlers, only to find themselves elbowed
aside, and later, shamefully subdued.

During the seventeenth century the men and women who

came to the colonies of the Atlantic shore in the greatest numbers were British, with a sprinkling of peoples from other
countries of Europe. They came singly, or in small groups, a
steady trickle that began to populate this vast continent. New
settlements were founded, colonies established. Everyone was
welcomed: Nobody bothered to count how many people arrived, or how many ships landed.

The resources of the new world seemed to be boundless;
the need was for more hands to exploit what the land had to
offer. Some settlers were so eager for help that they resorted to
buying other human beings. Men and women from Africa
were brought to this continent in chains and sold to landowners at public auction. This practice was so brutal and divisive
that its effects ravage our country to this day.

The forced immigration of African slaves differed in
most respects from the experience of men and women who
came on their own impulse. Within the context of this book, an
immigrant will be defined as one who chose to leave his home
and seek a new life in the United States.

After the colonies became a nation the flow of immigrants
began to increase, slowly at first, then in great surges. Since
1820, more than forty-four million people have come to the
United States to live and settle.

They have come from all over the world; they represent
all religious faiths. Once here, they have shared in every
phase of the building of the nation. They dug canals and laid
railroad tracks, built factories and houses. They washed
dishes, picked fruit, sewed clothes, mined gold, wrote songs,
broke virgin land out West.

Some immigrants have gone on to achieve great success in
business, government or the arts. The great majority have had
less spectacular careers: they have built a decent life for
themselves and their children, they have become an integral
part of America.

So much a part of this country have they become, that

today, a few generations after their arrival, we have almost forgotten their story. Nor has the story ended: New people are still coming to this country, as they did during all our yesterdays.

It would be impossible to relate all the experiences of the forty-four million who have come, or anticipate what will happen to those who will come in the future. But by following the saga of some of the major groups, we can hope to understand the total picture.

Who were the immigrants? Why did they come? These are questions we do not often ask ourselves. What did they leave behind in their homelands? And what did they find when they arrived? How did this country change them, and how did they change the country?

The reasons for their coming were as many and as varied as the people who came. Yet two causes were basic to all others: the immigrant was either escaping poverty, or searching for freedom. Or sometimes both.

He left behind the familiar landscape, often the language he had spoken since birth, the village where his people had lived for generations, to risk the fearful voyage, and the unknown shore.

At first, and sometimes for all his life, the newcomer was met by resentment, hostility and lack of understanding. His ways and language were ridiculed, he was greeted with offensive names. Those who had come before him coined such terms as mick and wop, bohunk and spick, kike, chink and dago. Each ugly word was purposely designed to make the new arrival feel scorned.

Having escaped from poverty, the immigrant most often found that the jobs open to him were lowest on the pay scale. In the new country his poverty was compounded by the agony of being a stranger, of no longer belonging to the community.

To ward off loneliness he tried to work with his own people, to live near those who spoke his language. Then slowly he began to overcome the obstacles, to take the first halting steps up the economic ladder, to create a life for himself and for his children in the larger community.

Then the space at the bottom of the ladder was taken by a new immigrant group. In the process, a new country was created.

For this *is* a new country, not only larger but in many ways different from the United States that existed before the great migrations began.

Before 1800 this was a nation patterned almost entirely on Great Britain. The people who came to the colonies, and then to the young republic, were largely English speaking and of the Protestant faith. More than 80 per cent of our population at that time was made up of people of British descent. When mass immigration began, men and women from the British Isles did not cease to cross the Atlantic, but their coming was overshadowed by the influx of millions from different cultures.

Today there is no majority group in our country; we are composed entirely of minorities.

Our speech is English, but peppered with phrases borrowed from dozens of languages. Our daily menus include dishes from all over the world. We worship in churches of all religions. The congressmen who represent us in Washington are drawn from all the various groups among us. Diversity is our pattern.

Often we are no longer aware of the origins of our institutions. The log cabin has become a symbol of pioneer America; we have forgotten that we learned how to build it from our Swedish ancestors. And that kindergarten—the first stepping-stone in our educational system—was brought by the Germans.

In an American schoolroom today, many students can not readily name the country of their origin. Fewer still can relate the circumstances of their ancestors' arrival.

"From what country did your people come?" a teacher asked her high school pupils.

"America," most of them replied.

But after consulting with their parents and grandparents they came back with some remarkable stories.

"One of my ancestors was a Hessian soldier," one girl related. "He came here to help the British put down the American Revolution. After the war was over, he decided this was a good place to settle."

"My grandfather came from Greece," said a boy. "There were too many children in his family, and not enough money; so he left home at the age of thirteen, with one of his brothers. They were supposed to join an uncle in Newark, New Jersey, but they took the wrong train, and wound up in Newark, Ohio."

"My mother left Germany in 1935 with her parents. They were escaping Hitler's persecution."

"My father's people came here from Sweden in 1830. They bought twelve acres of woodland in Minnesota for $100. They started a dairy farm."

The stories followed each other in rapid succession, each fascinating, each different.

We are all different from one another in background, heritage, traditions. The United States is woven of myriads of different threads, each adding its own characteristics—its strengths and weaknesses, talents and problems—to the fabric of the nation.

Settling the New Continent

To the shores of America, in its earliest days, came the explorers, followed in close succession by colonists and immigrants.

The explorers landed, took note of what was interesting in this uncharted land, then went back to the old world to describe their findings.

They came from Spain and Portugal, from Italy and France, from England, Russia and Scandinavia. Expeditions were often sponsored by rulers of one country and captained by men of another. Christopher Columbus, who was born in Italy and sailed under a Spanish flag, numbered among his crew members a Negro, an Englishman, an Irishman and a Jew. Captain Vitus Bering, who discovered that America and Asia are divided by water, was a Danish navigator in the service of the Russian crown. There was an international flavor to our country from its very start!

In some areas, expedition members stayed behind to start new settlements.

A Spanish expedition founded our first city in 1565: St. Augustine, in Florida. In the states of the Southwest many cities still bear Spanish names, such as Los Angeles, Santa Fe, Taos and Amarillo. Throughout that area one can still see evidence of Spanish architecture and customs, which were strengthened by a later influx of Spanish-speaking people.

French expeditions roamed through Maine and Vermont, the valley of the Ohio river and of the Mississippi.

"Voilà les mont verts!" Samuel de Champlain is thought to have said. "Behold the green mountains!" Vermont took its name from the words of the French explorer. In the bayous of Louisiana people still speak a dialect derived from the French.

For the most part, the explorers came and went. Even where they founded settlements, their influence remained local, never reaching across the continent.

It was the British colonists who came to the new land in the greatest numbers. It was they who gave it its original character.

Beginning in 1607 at Jamestown, Virginia, and in 1620 in Plymouth, Massachusetts, men and women from Great Britain built their communities in the image of the home country. English ways took hold very quickly. The English language, the laws, the forms of local self-government, town names, furniture styles, church hymns and nursery rhymes were quickly established in the early villages and accepted throughout the colonies.

English ways and institutions became official at the time the colonies declared themselves a nation. Though they have undergone considerable change, they remain the foundations of our society.

Of all the groups who came, early British settlers had the hardest and at the same time the easiest time adjusting to the new continent. The land was wild and dangerous, and taming it took many rugged years. But, because they were first, the English did not have to adapt their habits to those of other people. They suffered many physical privations, but they did not have to contend with the distrust and suspicion that greeted later groups.

When others followed, the process of adapting was easiest for those whose culture was most similar to the British, hardest for those who were most different.

While British citizens were developing large areas of Massachusetts and Virginia, the Dutch were settling the valley of the Hudson River and the area that is now New York City. They named it New Amsterdam. Before long they took over a section of Delaware Bay, which a Swedish party had unsuccessfully tried to colonize.

Although Dutch rule over the area lasted only some fifty years, its influence has endured. Along the banks of the Hudson one can still find a few fine mansions built in the 1600s by Dutch *patroons*, the landlords who held huge estates in the valley. The distinctive barns built by colonial Dutchmen, with large center doors, low eaves and gable ends, have been widely copied by succeeding generations of Americans. Place names that we consider English, such as Harlem or the Bowery, are in fact Dutch, as are all names ending in "kill," which meant creek: the town of Peekskill, the Catskill Mountains, the Schuylkill River.

One of our most beloved institutions, Santa Claus, was brought to the new world by Dutch colonists, as was the custom of exchanging visits on New Year's Day. Peter Minuit, who bought the island of Manahattan from the Indians for twenty-four dollars worth of goods, and Peter Stuyvesant, the last Dutch governor of New Amsterdam, are an integral part of the history of our country.

In 1664, Great Britain took over the Dutch colony. The Duke of York, who renamed New Amsterdam after himself, found it to be a gayer, brighter community than those of the Puritan English. Ladies and gentlemen wore colorful clothes in New Amsterdam, and games like bowling, backgammon

Wood engraving of New Year's Day in New Amsterdam about 1650.
Museum of the City of New York.

New Amsterdam, circa 1650-1653. The J. Clarence Davies Collection,
Museum of the City of New York.

and dice were freely played. It was a thriving, cosmopolitan colony in which eighteen different languages were spoken. Dutch governors, unable to recruit enough of their own countrymen, had welcomed people from all over the world.

By and large, the American colonies welcomed all men. But there were some that were not anxious for new settlers, the outstanding example being the Massachusetts colonies. Founded by Puritans, men and women who themselves had fled religious persecution, these settlements in turn denied admission to people of other persuasions. "Exceeding wedded to their own way" they were, according to an English merchant who visited the colonies.

From 1620 to 1641 some 20,000 British colonists came to New England. They believed in large families, and their own population increased at such a rate that they did not need, or want, additions from the outside.

Non-English-speaking groups seeking shelter in the new land were directed toward other areas, and many chose Pennsylvania.

William Penn advertised his colony widely, and let it be known throughout Central Europe that there would be no national or religious requirements for people wanting land. Himself a Quaker, a dissenter from the established religion of Great Britain, Penn wanted to provide a home for his own people and also for other groups fleeing their native country. In the seventeenth century, when a group left the old world, it was frequently for religious reasons.

The earlier split of some groups from the Catholic Church, which became known as the Reformation, had led to discontent and rebellion in large areas of Europe. People whose religion differed from that of their rulers were widely persecuted. Many began to look for a new country where they could practice their beliefs; to most, America seemed the best place in which to start anew.

Of these groups, several deserve a special mention because of their size, and because of the influence they exerted during colonial days.

First were the French Huguenots, who started arriving on this continent in 1660. When, in 1685, their right to worship as Protestants was officially denied by the Catholic king of France, some 15,000 Huguenots left their homeland.

Many were artisans and tradesmen, fairly cultured and well-to-do. They settled in towns throughout the colonies. A few were even welcomed in Massachusetts.

In Boston, the brothers Faneuil became prosperous merchants and built Faneuil Hall, which they presented to the city. It was meant as a market hall and meeting place; many secret gatherings that led to the Revolutionary War were held there. Today it is a major historical landmark; it was from Faneuil Hall that John F. Kennedy spoke to the American people on the eve of his election to the presidency in 1960.

A group of Huguenots founded New Rochelle in the colony of New York, naming it after La Rochelle, the French city where they were born. It became famous for its fine schools and fashionable young ladies and gentlemen from eastern colonies were sent there to learn the French language and etiquette.

The largest number of Huguenots settled in South Carolina. Many of the beautifully preserved homes in Charleston were built by them. The French came there on an equal footing with English settlers because the city was newly founded. They soon became influential and prosperous, keeping their French ways for quite some time.

In most colonies, the Huguenots rapidly shed their French characteristics and became Anglicized. A silversmith named Rivoire changed his name "merely on account that the bumpkins should pronounce it easier." His son was Paul Revere, patriot of the American Revolution.

From the German states came another large group fleeing religious persecution. There, Catholics and Protestants had clashed violently, and many decades of war had left misery and devastation.

Lured by William Penn's advertisement of his colony as a haven for dissenters, members of many different Protestant sects made their way to the harbors of Europe, and from there to Pennsylvania. There were among them Mennonites and Dunkards, Amish and Pietists, whose beliefs and customs were in some ways similar to those of the Quakers.

The first group of thirteen families reached Philadelphia in 1683 on the ship *Concord*, led by their minister, Franz Daniel Pastorius.

They named their original settlement Germantown, and by 1710 they were ready to hold their first annual fair. Pastorius, was teacher, minister, mayor and commercial developer. He taught his fellow townsmen to take advantage of the fertile soil; and they learned to raise flax and to weave linen, which they sold to the gentry in Philadelphia.

Germantown grew into a prosperous community, and became a way station through which most later immigrants from Germany passed. They stayed a while with their countrymen to rest from the arduous voyage, then traveled further, settling in the valleys of Pennsylvania and Delaware. By 1766, Benjamin Franklin told the Pennsylvania House of Commons, Germans made up one third of the population of the colony.

These early settlers of Pennsylvania are the forefathers of the people we mistakenly call Pennsylvania Dutch: They were not Hollanders, but *Deutsch*, or German.

Most of them in time blended into the life of the colony and adopted English as their language. Not so the members of the separatist sects, or "sectarians." There were some thirty of these sects in Lancaster County alone. Although there were differences among the various groups, they held in common a desire to live separate lives, to be left alone to practice their beliefs. Pacifist in outlook, they refused to bear arms during

Bittet aber, daß eure Flucht nicht geschehe im Winter, oder am Sabbath. Matt. 24. v. 2

Salzburgische Emigranten.

Nichts, als das Evangelium
Vertreibt uns ins Exilium,
Verlaßen wir das Vaterland,
So sind wir doch in Gottes Hand.

Die Hoch Fürstliche Haupt und Residenz STADT SALZBURG, von Mitternacht anzusehen.

Erklärung der Ziffern.	4. Uhralt Cl. S. Peter O.S. Ben:	7. Bürger Spittal zum H. Geist	11. H.F. Lust Palast und Welt	14. Aller Heil: Dreyfaltigkeit
Haupt Vest Hohen Salzb	5. Franciscaner Closter.	8. Ursulinerinnen zu S. Marx	scher Garten Mirabell.	Kirch u. Virgilian Colleg.
Ertz Bischöfl: Thumkirche	6. Ben: Universit. mit der	9. Augustiner Closter.	12. Graff Lodron: Pallast.	15. Capuciner Closter. 16. S. Sebastian Bruderhaus
Hoch Fürstl. Residentz	Prächt: Kirche Im: C.B.V.M	10. Das Rathhaus.	13. Lodronisches Collegium	der Freydhof, wo Theophr. Pa= racelsus begraben liegt.

German immigrants from Salzburg in 1732. Library of Congress.

the Revolutionary War. But many helped the cause of their adopted country by doing hospital work.

The sectarians have kept unchanged their habits, appearance, speech and religious beliefs to a degree unmatched in the rest of the United States. They were, and still are, hard-working, simple-living farmers. Two and a half centuries after their arrival, some of them still scorn cars and drive black horse-drawn carriages. They wear plain black clothes; the men grow beards; the women are never seen without a bonnet. They pass their customs from one generation to another by intermarrying and by refusing to let their children attend public schools. Many still speak their own language, a distinctive mixture of German and English.

One of the most important contributions of the Pennsylvania Dutch to American history was the manufacture of the first covered wagons in Conestoga, Pennsylvania. They used their wagons as "ships of inland commerce," to transport the produce of their fields to nearby markets. In the following century the Conestoga wagons became the major means of westward travel for the pioneers.

The third sizeable group that immigrated during colonial days is known today as Scotch-Irish, although in the early 1700s, when most of them arrived, they were referred to as Irish. The hyphen was added later to differentiate them from the Catholic Irish who immigrated in the nineteenth century.

The Scotch-Irish had lived in Northern Ireland for several generations. Their forefathers had been Presbyterians, who had come there from Scotland.

One hundred years of clearing forests, farming and weaving in Ireland had brought them scant reward. Conditions were dismal for everyone on the island, but the Presbyterians had the greatest problems. Their civil rights were severely curtailed; they could not hold office nor run their own schools.

Returning to Scotland was out of the question; their ties to that country were long gone. And since they were descendents of settlers and frontiersmen, the vastness of the new world held great appeal.

Landing in Philadelphia or Baltimore with very little money, they made their way to places where land was free: the forests and valleys of western Pennsylvania, the Shenandoah Valley, the unsettled areas of Virginia and the Carolinas.

Once the land was cleared, they often sold it to later immigrants and moved on. During the nineteenth century, as the westward movement gained momentum, they were in the vanguard of the pioneers.

As settlers in Ireland, the Scotch-Irish had known little peace. They had become a rough and daring people, opponents of the established order, always ready for a fight, ideal frontiersmen. They had suffered privations because of their religion, and it had become a unifying force among them. Their ministers followed close behind the first settlers, working with plow and axe when they were not preaching fiery sermons.

It was the preachers who were in charge of instructing the young; and as soon as possible they started small academies, some of which turned into fine schools and universities. Princeton University was founded in 1746 by Scottish Presbyterian ministers. Thirty years later, Princeton President John Witherspoon was the only clergyman among the signers of the Declaration of Independence.

The influence of the Scotch-Irish on our early history was far-reaching, strengthening the British character of the colonies. Because they scattered throughout the land, and were not hampered by having to learn a new language, they carried their religion and traditions far and wide. In some mountain valleys of Kentucky and Tennessee, isolated from urban civilization, descendents of Scotch-Irish pioneers still preserve customs and folk songs of their ancestors.

It was once thought that all early immigrants from Ireland were of the Presbyterian faith, but later research has proved that there were Catholics among them. Whatever their religious persuasion, colonial records refer to them as Irish. Being anti-British by tradition, they all joined the American Revolution in large numbers and with enthusiasm. St. Patrick's Day was observed throughout the revolutionary army by orders of General George Washington.

There were other Europeans who came singly or in small units to the American colonies.

Individual Englishmen kept coming, although they attracted less attention. They were people seeking a brighter future in the new land, lawyers, doctors and artisans, or younger sons of noble families who would not be inheriting land and title.

Often, there was sharp competition among the colonies for immigrants whose skills were considered desirable. Master craftsmen were eagerly sought, as well as artisans of all kinds. Farmers who could start specific projects were invited by individual colonies to come with their families or to come in an entire community.

Musicians, artists and professional people were welcome in all the cities, as were the writers and scholars who came to study the American experiment.

A sizeable percentage of the newcomers were set apart from these, however, by the circumstances of their arrival. They were indentured servants, people who sold themselves into temporary servitude in order to come to America.

Most indentured servants were British, but there were some from Germany and Ireland. They were people whose financial situation was so desperate that they would pledge themselves for a number of years in order to have a chance at a better life.

At times they knew who their buyer would be before they left Europe. Others were sold at auction when their boat reached an American harbor.

In colonial newspapers, one would frequently read an advertisement such as this:

"Just imported from Dublin . . . a parcel of Irish servants, both men and women, to be sold cheap."

Or one announcing:

"A parcel of choice Scotch servants, taylors, weavers, shoemakers and ploughmen, some for five and others for seven years . . ."

Schoolmasters were advertised, too, often at a lower price than craftsmen.

Adults were "bound out" for three to six years, boys and girls from ten to fifteen.

The main difference between indenture and slavery was that, for the first, there was a time limit, a day in sight when freedom would come. For the true slaves, the African men and women kidnapped and forcibly brought over to be sold, the day of liberty was far slower in coming.

At the end of the period of indenture the servant was released from his contract, given a suit of clothes, a predetermined amount of money, and the right of free citizenship.

A typical contract might read as this one:

"Eva Wagner, with consent of her father, to John M. Brown of Northern Libertyes, Philadelphia Country, Riger, for five years, to have six months' schooling and at the end of the term two complete suits of clothes, one of which to be new, also 1 straw bed, 1 bedstead, 1 blanket, 1 pillow, 1 sheet. 70 Dollars."

Once their term was completed, little prejudice was held against former indentured servants. They took their place in the life of the colony according to their abilities, and many became eminent citizens.

Among the signers of the Declaration of Independence there were two, Matthew Thornton of New Hampshire and George Taylor of Pennsylvania, who had come from Ireland and spent some years as indentured servants.

They were the forerunners of millions of Irish men and women who reached America's shores after the colonies became a nation, forming the first great wave of immigration.

"Why the Irish Came to America"

IN IRISH HOMES, they tell a special story called "Why the Irish Came to America." The hero is a foreign king who is being stalked by Death. Clever and wily, the king convinces Death to step into a box. Then he closes the lid, drops the box into the sea, and returns to his far-away home.

"The box floated a long time in the ocean," the tale continues, "till it came to Ireland and was washed ashore. Men got the box up on the shore and began to wonder what was in it. Two big Irishmen got sledge hammers and broke the box open. Death flew out and . . . started to killin' people all over Ireland. That was why the Irishmen left Ireland and came to America."

For the Irish of the nineteenth century it must have been easy to imagine that Death itself was at work in their land. Almost a million people died between 1845 and 1850, the years of the potato famine. And another million emigrated to America. In five years, Ireland lost one quarter of its population.

For many centuries the great majority of Irish people had lived in abject poverty. In the late 1500s the potato was brought to Europe from South America, and from that time on the average Irishman's daily diet had consisted of potatoes, with a little salt, washed down with skimmed milk. They boiled the potatoes, then peeled the skin off with a thumbnail overgrown especially for that purpose. "The bit and the sup," the meal was called. When times were hard, an unsalted potato was the entire meal, and water the drink.

A succession of cold, damp summers brought about a plant disease known as potato rot. Whole crops were destroyed overnight.

Years later a young Irishman recalled that he had gone to the mountains one afternoon in the fall of 1845, passing fields solidly planted with potatoes. Coming back early the next morning, "he felt a peculiar smell," he said. It was the odor of the potato blight. One day the stalks were green and healthy, the next day "they were as black as your shoe and burned to the clay."

Other crops were not affected. But most people had survived on potatoes, and they starved. Beggars crowded country roads and city streets, livestock perished, disease ravaged the island.

In 1847, a young English Quaker described the Irish town of Westport with these words:

"A strange and fearful sight, like what we read of in beleaguered cities; its streets crowded with gaunt wanderers, sauntering to and fro with hopeless air and hunger-struck look —a mob of starved, almost naked women around the poorhouse clamoring for soup tickets . . ."

"The weekly returns of the dead were like the bulletin of a fierce campaign," remarked a current publication.

This disaster had hit a country already weakened by adversity.

For hundreds of years, foreign invaders had raided Irish

Distribution of clothing to poverty-stricken Irish at Kilrush.

Irish immigrants leaving home.

soil. Since 1169 the kings of England had considered it their domain. Ireland was conquered territory, bound to England by a series of laws that denied its people every right. Irish Catholics could not own land, vote or attend school. And they had to pay a tax for the support of the Church of England, which they hated.

Conditions grew progressively worse over the centuries, and reached their ebb in the eighteen hundreds. By then, most Irishmen lived on the land, in utter poverty.

Since schools were forbidden, illiteracy was almost total. The few who could read had learned the alphabet from the village priest or from a "hedge school-teacher": a man who taught in secret, hiding in the peasant's hut or behind a roadside hedge.

Rebellions flared up periodically in one or another section of the island, only to be brutally extinguished. Ruled by force, the Irish replied with force.

Secret organizations flourished in city and country. There were groups known as Ribbonmen, Whiteboys, Levellers, Molly Maguires. Whatever their local name, the basic purpose of the organization was to protect the peasantry. If a landlord was unduly harsh to his tenants, the secret society would meet to judge him: their course of action often involved blackmail, beatings and murder.

The only institution that the Irish peasant felt truly belonged to him was the Catholic Church, and it was to the Church that he gave his unquestioned loyalty. It was a poor Church, dependent on the small contributions of its members.

The priest was friend and protector to the peasants; it was to him that they turned in sickness, or for advice on daily problems. It was he who helped them find what meaning was possible in their lives.

It was into this world, unchanged for hundreds of years, that the potato famine of 1845 swept. When it came there was no choice for hundreds of thousands but to perish or leave.

Since the beginning of the first settlements, America had held great appeal for the Irish. There were many songs that expressed this feeling. One of the most popular went:

> With my bundle on my shoulder,
> Sure, there's no man could be bolder:
> I'm leavin' dear old Ireland without warnin'
> For I lately took the notion,
> For to cross the briny ocean,
> And I'm off for Philadelphia in the mornin'.

For many, passage money came from American building companies, eager for cheap labor. For many more, from friends and relatives in the United States. English relief funds helped some, although the efforts of the British government have largely been forgotten, while the help that came from the United States is remembered to this day.

The roads to Irish ports became crowded with ragged, barefoot families, pushing wheelbarrows that held their few possessions. If a man had shoes he carried them in his hand to save them for the journey. When the children grew weary they took turns at riding on the wheelbarrow.

Some people boarded ships at Cork, others crossed to England and boarded at Liverpool. Once they reached the port town there was often a delay of many days while the captain waited for his freight to arrive. By the time the cargo was loaded many immigrant families had already spent whatever meager funds they had.

On the day of departure, they would pile into the steerage section of the boat with their food and possessions, a few cooking utensils, and often a small cloth bundle containing a precious handful of earth to remind them of home.

How often they thought of home during the four to ten weeks of the journey can only be imagined. For many, the horrors of the famine must have paled compared to those of the voyage. No ocean crossing was easy or pleasant in the middle of the nineteenth century, but the ones from Liverpool were said to have been the worst.

There was no limit then to the number of passengers that could be herded into a ship, or to the amount of cargo. At times the boat was so overloaded that it foundered and sank in bad weather. Shipowners were heavily insured, however, and continued to send out their "coffin ships."

Despite several acts passed by the Congress of the United States to regulate conditions on immigrant ships, it was only when steamships came into general use that any real improvement was possible. In the old sailing vessels, immigrants were housed in steerage quarters five feet high which held two tiers of bunks. Fresh air came in only through the hatches; and they had to be closed during storms, when fresh air was most needed.

There were fair days as well as foul, of course, and if the captain was a decent man he might allow his passengers to dance a few jigs and reels to the tune of a fiddle. In sunny weather, the immigrants sometimes sat on the main deck, singing an old favorite, or one of the more recent ballads that told of people like themselves.

> Oh, the times are hard and the wages are low,
>   Amelia, where you bound for?
> Across the ocean we must go,
>   Across the ocean we must go.

> Beware these packet ships, I say,
>   Amelia, where you bound for?
> They'll steal your stores and clothes away
>   Across the ocean we must go.

> It was rotten meat and weevily bread,
>   Amelia, where you bound for?

Panoramic painting by Samuel B. Waugh of immigrants landing
in the Battery in 1855. Museum of the City of New York.

> Eat it or starve, the captain said,
> Across the ocean we must go.
>
> Oh, the winds were foul and the times were hard,
> Amelia, where you bound for?
> From Liverpool dock to the Brooklyn yard,
> Across the ocean we must go.

Steerage passengers were expected to bring and cook their own food; a tiny room was set aside as a galley, and everyone took turns. Nobody ever managed to get the food more than half cooked, and provisions usually spoiled long before the end of the journey.

Diseases of all kinds broke out: "Ship fever" (typhus), cholera, dysentery, "rotten-throat." The death rate at sea was at times as high as 15 per cent. Water was always rationed. On a good trip, no one went thirsty; but there was never enough water for washing. Passengers landed in America covered with sores and scabs.

There, they were examined by a doctor, who might say with a sneer:

"In America, we bathe!"

And respectable newspapers greeted the newcomers with words like these:

"The lowest order of humanity . . . filthy in their habits, coarse in manner, and often low in their instincts."

It was fortunate that most of them could not read. For the Irish had landed in a country that resented them bitterly and had no idea of the contribution they were to make to its development.

For all the misery and suffering of the voyage, most of the passengers considered themselves fortunate; what mattered to them was that they were landing in a country where jobs were plentiful, where a man had but to work and he would not starve.

Many kissed the ground as they came ashore; some

spilled on American soil the bit of earth they had brought from home. They did not know how long it would be before this symbolic gesture could become a reality.

Before the famine years, early in the nineteenth century, immigrants coming from Ireland had been small businessmen and farmers. They were ambitious people, with some education; they had settled in many different areas of the United States and had found comparatively little resistance from other inhabitants. But the famine years changed all that.

"Thousands continually land entirely penniless and are at once in a state of destitution," read a pamphlet published by an Irish emigrant society of New York, "whereas each person should have at least five pounds on his arrival to enable him to prosecute his journey to the interior."

It was wise advice, but most of the newcomers were unable to heed it. The new immigrants, who were rural people back home, became city dwellers in the United States. There simply was no money with which to continue the journey once they reached the seacoast cities.

They landed in New York, Boston and Philadelphia, and there they stayed.

When an Irishman arrived he usually moved into one of the many boarding houses run by his countrymen. It was always overcrowded, and he was almost certainly fleeced. Later, he would discover that there was little in the way of permanent housing he could afford. Owners were charging handsome rentals for attics, cellars, warehouses. Sometimes twenty families would move into one house; an entire family would share one room without light or ventilation.

In an attempt to recreate the neighborliness of the village back home, Irish immigrants moved close to each other. On Saturday nights, the new arrivals—they were called "greenhorns"—were welcomed at a "kitchen racket" in the tenement home of an Irish friend. The women exchanged advice; the men helped each other find jobs.

There were plenty of openings for the women; Irish girls

were much in demand as household helpers and nursemaids. Generations of American children fell asleep to the sound of Irish songs and fairy tales.

The men had no education and no skills to offer a prospective employer. But they had muscle power and the kind of stamina born of centuries of hard physical work. They arrived as the industrial revolution was starting to change the American pattern of living. And they took over the physical building of the country.

They built houses, streets, sewers and water supply systems. They dug ditches and loaded ships. They built canals all along the East Coast; and when the canals were finished, they joined in the frantic building of railroads. "There's an Irishman buried under every railroad tie," people used to say.

"Paddy Works on the Railroad" is a song that has remained popular to this day.

> In eighteen hundred and forty-one
> I put my cord'roy breeches on,
> Put my cord'roy breeches on
> To work upon the railway.
>
> Billy meoo, re-eye, re-aye,
> Billy meoo, re-eye, re-aye,
> Billy meoo, re-eye, re-aye,
> To work upon the railway.
>
> In eighteen hundred and forty-two,
> I left the ould world for the new,
> Bad 'cess to the luck that brought me through,
> To work upon the railway.
>
> *Chorus*
>
> When we left Ireland to come here
> And spend our latter days in cheer,

Our bosses, they did drink strong beer,
And we worked on the railway.

Chorus

Our contractor's name it was Tom King.
He kept a store to rob the men,
A Yankee clerk with ink and pen
To cheat Pat on the railway.

Chorus

It's "Pat, do this," and "Pat, do that!"
Without a stocking or a hat,
And nothing but an old cravat,
While Pat works on the railway.

Chorus

One Monday morning to our surprise,
Just half an hour before sunrise,
The dirty divil went to the skies,
And Pat worked on the railway.

Chorus

Paddy was the name by which Americans knew the Irish newcomer. His working day started before dawn and ended after dark. He worked for a dollar a day. To a greenhorn that sounded like a great deal; but in time he learned that he must purchase his food at the company store, where prices were outrageous. And often part of his wage was paid in a daily ration of whiskey.

Injuries and accidents were frequent in road building and canal digging. The labor camps to which the men returned at night were run-down shanties, torn by frequent brawls. No man wanted his family living there. And still the Irish immigrants kept coming. Contractors hired them right off the boats, offering them the lowest possible pay, undercutting the wages of their countrymen already at work. Fights often broke out, sometimes just a brief flare-up, other times a major riot like the one on the Chesapeake and Ohio Canal. President Jackson had to use federal troops to break up that battle.

Native Americans disapproved and criticized the bloody spirit of the Irish worker, but in almost every case the riots were caused by unbearable working and living conditions. To cope with the injustices they suffered, the Irish workmen sometimes employed the methods of violence and secrecy they had mastered in the old country. There were secret societies among laborers in various areas despite attempts by the Church and the more responsible citizens to discourage their activities. The most powerful and most infamous took its name directly from one of the groups in Ireland, the Molly Maguires.

For more than a decade, the Molly Maguires terrorized the anthracite coal mining region of Pennsylvania. In the valleys of the Allegheny mountains, mine laborers lived like slaves, and worked as hard. Over 50 percent of the men were Irish; the others—the English, Scottish and Welsh—had arrived first, and held slightly better jobs. Early, peaceful attempts at protesting working conditions met with reprisals from the mine owners. So the movement fell into the hands of criminals.

By the 1860s the influence of the Molly Maguires could be felt throughout the region. The mine bosses were the chosen victims: They were blackmailed and murdered; their homes and offices were burned. Local officials were elected or defeated according to the wishes of the Molly Maguires. Everyone lived in terror. And no one knew who the Molly Maguires were.

Then management hired a young detective fresh from Ireland, James McParlan. For two years he posed as a friend of the miners. He joined their organizations, listened to their problems, sang and danced to their tunes, even helped plan violence against the bosses.

In 1875, his disclosures led to a series of trials after which nineteen men were hanged. Afterwards, no one was quite sure that the right men had been killed, because the trials had been held in an atmosphere of prejudice and hysteria. But the power of the Molly Maguires was broken. And the scandalous conditions under which miners worked and lived had been exposed to the public.

Twenty-five years later, when the United Mine Workers of America was finally recognized by management, its president was another Irishman, John Mitchell.

In his honor, a miner composed a ballad that was to be sung in broken English:

> Righta here I'm tella you,
> Me no scabby fella,
> Me good union citizen,
> Me Johnny Mitchell man.

Meanwhile work progressed on canals and railroads, and many of the workers settled along the right-of-way. In Lowell, Massachusetts, for example, the first Irish laborers arrived in 1822 to build a canal. In the beginning they lived in "Paddy Camp Lands," then later in a group of cabins known as New Dublin. Soon a small Catholic church went up, and the workers' families came from the tenements of the big cities to join their men. Once the canal was completed, many of the men got jobs in local textile mills; the migrant Irish laborer had become a permanent citizen.

This process was repeated in numerous New England towns, and elsewhere on the Atlantic coast. By following a map of public improvement projects—canals, railroads, mill races—one can trace the development of Irish-American communities in the United States.

None of it happened painlessly. Far from it. Since the Irish were the first of the great surges of immigrants to reach these shores, they were also first to endure discrimination. Settled Americans were caught unawares: Never had they been faced with such an overwhelming group of people so unlike themselves. "No Irish Need Apply" was a sign that hung outside numerous homes and places of business.

The immigrants' poverty made them eager for any sort of work at any kind of pay. Older Americans feared the economic competition, although they were not eager to do the pick and shovel work themselves. The immigrants' poverty caused them to live in substandard surroundings; they were blamed for the hovels in which they lived, and the disorder they created.

Then there was the matter of the immigrants' religion. The United States had been created largely as a haven for dissident Protestants; few Catholics had lived here before the 1840s. The militant Catholicism of the Irish masses was hard for Protestants to accept.

Nobody knows who the instigators were, but it is a fact that in most major cities, riots and fights broke out between American Protestants and Irish Catholics.

In Boston, a convent school was burned to the ground. In Dorchester, Massachusetts, a Catholic church was blown up. And in Philadelphia, one of the bloodiest riots in the city's history broke out in 1844 when Bishop Kenrick objected to having Catholic children read a Protestant Bible in school. Nativist mobs stormed the Catholic section of the city, setting fire to Catholic homes and yelling "God, Country and Bible."

One of the most controversial issues of the time was a book published in New York in 1836, entitled *The Awful Disclosures of Maria Monk*. It was supposed to be the autobiography of a young nun, and was filled with scandalous accounts of life behind the walls of a convent. Shortly after publication, the author's mother disclosed that the story was a complete lie; meanwhile, it had sold more than 300,000 copies.

Secret societies began to gather strength in all the major cities to fight the influence of the "foreigners." At first the groups were independent of each other, but gradually they merged into a powerful political party.

Officially, it was known as the "American party." Whenever anyone asked about its program members were instructed to reply "I know nothing about it." Soon they became known as the Know-Nothings. In mysterious ceremonies, complete with passwords, signs and ritual grips, members swore to vote only for native Americans, to fight Catholicism and to demand a twenty-one year naturalization period for all foreigners.

The Know-Nothings revealed their allegiance only to each other, with the following signal: A member would close one *eye*, form the letter *o* with his thumb and forefinger and place it over his *nose*. *Eye, nose, zero* meant *I Know Nothing*.

For almost a decade, the Know-Nothings wielded extraordinary influence. At the height of their power—in the mid 1850s—they elected governors in six different states, seventy-five representatives to Congress and nominated their own candidate for President.

A century later, President John F. Kennedy commented:

"The Irish are perhaps the only people in our history with the distinction of having a political party formed against them."

As mysteriously as they came to power, the Know-Nothings suddenly faded away. Few of their aims had actually been achieved; the tide of immigration rose after the middle of the century, and Irish political power increased. But by 1860 the United States had turned its attention to another issue, one that was to split it apart: slavery.

The Civil War caught the American Irish in a dilemma. For decades the debate over abolition had been heard in the land. The Irish immigrant, never a friend to the Negro, was opposed to freeing the slaves. He feared the economic competition. As longshoremen, as manual laborers, it was Negroes and Irishmen who vied for the jobs. The Irish worried that freed slaves would come North in large numbers and lower wages. They also felt that their own lot was similar to that of the slaves. Northerners should concern themselves with the problems at hand, many said, before righting those of the South. The Irish were too new, too insecure in their position in their adopted country, to favor abolition.

Yet when war was declared, the Irish immediately rallied to President Lincoln's call. Their allegiance to the cause of the Union, to the American form of government, was unquestioned. Besides, they loved a good fight!

170,000 Irishmen fought in the Union Army. Irish brigades flew the Irish flag alongside the Stars and Stripes; Irish officers were in command; and Irish priests went along to comfort the men. Some soldiers were recruited while still in Ireland; others as they poured off the boats in New York harbor.

Bloody and divisive as the Civil War was, it served to bring together Catholics and Protestants in an effort to preserve the Union.

Late in the war, an Irish flag bearer named Mike Scannel was captured at Petersburg.

"Hand over those colors, Yankee," ordered a Confederate soldier, pointing a pistol at Mike.

"Yankee is it, now," replied Mike as he handed over the flag. "Faith, I've been twenty years in this country and nobody ever paid me the compliment before."

But before the conflict was over, one of the most painful episodes in the history of the American Irish took place in New York City: the draft riots.

In January of 1863 President Lincoln issued the Emancipation Proclamation. Freedom from slavery had become an official aim of the war. It was an aim to which most American Irish were still opposed.

Wood engraving from *The Illustrated London News*, 1864, of the
enlisting in the U.S. Army of Irish and German immigrants
in New York. Museum of the City of New York.

Volunteer enlistments in the Union Army fell off sharply. In need of soldiers, the government decreed that all able-bodied men must serve in the army or pay $300 in cash. The rich could avoid fighting; for the struggling Irish, there was no escaping the draft.

The Irish erupted. For three days, gangs of infuriated men terrorized New York. They marched into Central Park and burned down the draft office. They looted the homes of the wealthy on Lexington Avenue, raided stores, overturned carriages, tore down a Negro orphanage. A number of Negroes were lynched. Throughout the three days, rioters fought bitterly against the police, most of whom were Irish, too.

Finally federal troops brought order to the city, and Archbishop Hughes, an Irishman and a friend of Lincoln's, held a mass meeting outside his house, calling upon his people to stop the violence.

The reputation of the Irish was damaged throughout the nation, despite the fact that most were law-abiding citizens who had not been involved at all.

Nor did the Civil War end the Irish involvement in war and fighting. There were other causes that appealed to the Irish soldier. Foremost among these was the liberation of his homeland from the hated British.

By the end of the Civil War there were thousands of trained, seasoned fighting men whose love for Ireland had never faded. And there were many Irish community leaders anxious to make use of these fighting skills.

In Ireland, a revolutionary organization had been founded aiming to form an Irish Republic. The American branch of this group became known as the Fenian Brotherhood, after a legendary hero known as Finn.

Thousands of Irish-Americans, civilians as well as Army and Navy men, joined the movement, pledging themselves to freedom for Ireland. A convention of Fenians in Cincinnati created on paper an Irish Republic, naming a president, a secretary of war and a full slate of officers. Their plan was to declare war on Great Britain; and they expected full support from the United States government. After all, hadn't they helped defend the Union?

What followed reads like a plot for light opera. The Fenians openly mapped their strategy, raising large sums of money with picnics and bond selling drives; servant girls and laborers gladly contributed their savings. Various plans of attack were discussed throughout the winter of 1866. Finally it was decided to invade Canada. If they took Canada, the Fenians figured, they could then swap it for Ireland.

The United States complied to an astonishing degree. Arms were being stored, men were converging toward the Canadian border; if the government knew about it, it did not let on. On the night of May 31, 1866, the people of Buffalo, N.Y., came down to the river to see an army of six hundred men crossing to Canada. There were supposed to be more, but some had indulged in too much celebration. On the opposite shore a few Canadians watched in amazement as boatloads of armed men landed on their soil and planted the Irish flag.

At this point President Andrew Johnson became nervous, and the Canadian garrisons woke up. A number of battles took place; the Fenians fought bravely, but by then the government had stopped their reinforcements from leaving United States soil. The Fenian army was forced to withdraw, and on its return to Buffalo it was marched off to jail.

Suddenly a storm of protest broke out in the United States. The British government protested that the United States had allowed the invasion to take place. The Fenians protested that they had been betrayed. Politicians interested in the Irish vote protested because so many men had been arrested, and demanded that they be released. They were, and were returned to their homes at government expense.

Other Americans, baffled by the entire episode, argued at length over the two conclusions they had to draw: The American Irish had achieved a great degree of political power; and the average Irishman, in spite of his new home, was still interested in the freedom of his homeland. He remained interested until the Republic of Ireland finally came into being in 1932.

The development of Irish political power was a gradual thing, but it had begun with the very first shiploads of immigrants. Poor and illiterate as they were, they landed with several built-in advantages over later groups of newcomers: They spoke English, and they were somewhat acquainted with Anglo-Saxon culture. There were some among them who realized the importance of voting as a group in order to fulfill their needs.

In New York, Boston, Philadelphia, the Irish formed their own tightly knit communities. With their meager savings, they built churches, and schools where their children could be brought up in the old faith. There was always a saloon nearby to which they could escape from their overcrowded quarters.

In these compact communities it was not difficult to form a political club. The club provided the services a newcomer needed: a job, the advice of a lawyer, guidance at city hall, a letter written for one who lacked the skill.

An ambitious young man could gain the everlasting loyalty of the group by performing such favors; he would be rewarded at election time. On riverboat excursions, or picnics with plenty of beer, a young politician would make a speech championing the causes dear to the heart of his listeners: stable wages, shorter hours, a vote for every citizen.

Politics became an attractive career for many young Irishmen, and one for which they were well suited by nature. Wit, a gift for speaking, a sensitivity to human needs, were qualities many of them possessed. And politics did not need long, technical training, which they could not afford. If a man was willing to start on a low level, he could go far.

The Irish plunged into American political life faster than any other immigrant group. Their desire for self-rule, so long denied in Ireland, came to the fore in their adopted country. They fought to break down the power of the majority, which would have liked to exclude them; in every voting district, they built their own organization.

Each new arrival was enlisted in the organization, and was made a citizen and a voter as soon as possible. There were instances in which "as soon as possible" was interpreted too literally. Americans bristled as they read of thousands of Irishmen being made voters by judges who asked no questions, provided the applicant was sponsored by the right party boss.

In New York City, a man could become a citizen in any of a number of places, including saloons. He would bring in a note from the organization leader that read, "Please naturalize the bearer", he would put his signature, or an x, on a piece of paper, and lo and behold, he was a citizen and voter.

The *New York Tribune* sneered:

"It is rumored that Judge McCunn has issued an order naturalizing all the lower counties of Ireland, beginning at Tipperary and running down to Cork. Judge Barnard will arrange for the northern counties at the next sitting of the chambers."

In the 1840s Tammany Hall, the oldest political club in New York City, and one that had been the most exclusive, began to court Irish immigrants. By 1880, New York City elected its first Irish mayor, William R. Grace. By the end of the nineteenth century, most big city government was in the hands of Irish politicians.

By the late nineteenth century, also, the pick and shovel had been handed over to the immigrant of a more recent wave. The Irish-American had become foreman of the construction gang, contractor, or often head of a construction company.

Charitable institutions and social clubs blossomed in all

the major Irish communities. The middle classes were eager to pattern themselves on older Americans.

A special target of Irish resentment late in the century were the many Irish plays and songs that were popular at the time. The Ancient Order of Hybernians, a powerful organization, organized a campaign to abolish the "stage Irishman." Dressed in a long-tailed coat and patched knee corduroys, clay pipe in his hat and a shillelah in his hand, speaking only the broadest brogue and using many uncouth words, the comic Irishman had been the focus of hundreds of plays, both comic and dramatic. In the 1850s, American audiences applauded such plays as "Ireland and America," "Ireland as It Is," "Irish Blunders of Handy Andy," "Irish Assurance and Yankee Modesty," "The Irish Thrush and the Swedish Nightingale."

The "lace curtain" Irish wanted to forget their past. In 1890, Edward Harrigan, who had written numerous plays, produced his last success, "Reilly and the Four Hundred." In it he satirized his newly wealthy countrymen with a song that said:

> There's an organ in the parlor to give the
>   house a tone,
> And you're welcoming every evening at Maggie
>   Murphy's home.

Irish plays as such soon disappeared from the American stage, but Irish influence on our theater and our popular music endures to this day. Irish songs have always been popular in America, from "Harrigan" to "Sweet Rosie O'Grady" and that favorite of New York politicians, "Sidewalks of New York."

Dublin-born Victor Herbert was in his time the most renowned bandmaster in America. He was also composer of such successful operettas as "Babes in Toyland," "The Red Mill"

Cover from sheet music of *Peg O' My Heart*, an Irish-based comedy performed in the early 1900's. Courtesy of Marguerite Courtney.

and "Naughty Marietta."

Yet it was through their involvement in politics and city government that the Irish made most of their contacts with other Americans. For the immigrant groups who arrived at the end of the century, the Irish were a bridge on which to cross to American life. It was the Irish policeman, the Irish fireman, the Irish politician to whom the Italian and the Russian newcomer turned when he needed help.

For many decades, Irish politicians limited themselves to local problems, to running wards, districts or cities, without any wider aspirations. The first man who rose beyond the city level was Alfred E. Smith.

Son of impoverished immigrants, Al Smith started his career delivering fish at Fulton Fish Market and became governor of the state of New York. He was a fighter for social welfare; a colorful, humorous speaker; the first leader of national caliber to emerge from immigrant slums.

He never forgot his own beginnings, nor did he try to hide them. At a hearing on opening several Long Island beaches to the public, Smith heard a landowner express fear that "the rabble" would be attracted to the area.

"Hey!" cried the Governor, "Rabble! I am the rabble!"

His schooling had ended at grammar school, but Al Smith educated himself for the state legislature and then the governorship.

"If you doubt the value of education," he used to say, "ask the man who never had one."

To help the lot of people who lived as he once had, he joined with social reformers in creating much needed legislation. He was considered an outstanding governor, but when the Democratic party nominated him for President in 1928, a wave of anti-Catholicism swept the country.

It was perhaps true that he lacked sufficient knowledge of national affairs, that the city and the state had been his special field, but it was bigotry that finally defeated him. His opponents even revived that best seller of 1836, *The Awful Disclosures of Maria Monk!*

The American Irish thought they had completed their Americanization. They were stunned by the set-back. It seemed impossible that a candidate's religion should remain an important consideration in an American election.

In 1960, John F. Kennedy, first Catholic to run for President since Al Smith, decided to face the issue head on. Before an audience of three hundred Protestant ministers, he discussed his religion and his beliefs. He spoke at length of the kind of America he envisioned:

"An America where religious intolerance will some day end, where every man has the same right to attend or not to attend the church of his choice, where there is no Catholic vote, no anti-Catholic vote, no bloc voting of any kind."

And he concluded:

"If I should lose on the real issues, I shall return to my seat in the Senate, satisfied that I tried my best and was fairly judged.

"But if this election is decided on the basis that 40,000,000 Americans lost their chance of being President on the day they were baptized, then it is the whole nation that will be the loser in the eyes of Catholics and non-Catholics around the world, in the eyes of history, and in the eyes of our own people."

On November 8, 1960, John F. Kennedy, great-grandson of an Irish immigrant, became President of the United States.

In the history of the American Irish, a new day had begun.

Mass Migration from Germany

IN 1847, A GERMAN IMMIGRANT in Wooster, Ohio, cut down a young spruce tree in the forest and brought it home to his family at Christmas time. There, with the help of his children and wife, he trimmed it with candles and paper decorations, as was the custom in his native land.

It may have been the first Christmas tree in the United States. Within a few years, cut spruces could be bought on the streets of most major cities. The tradition came into popular usage in the 1850s, when the tide of German immigration to America began to reach full force. Before that time, some Americans did not even stop working on Christmas. Puritan and Quaker beliefs frowned on any celebration of the day.

Certainly the coming of the Germans changed the American way of life during the month of December. How much more their coming changed America, most people no longer even realize.

One quarter of the population of the United States today is of German or part German descent. More German speaking people came to this country than any group except the British: over six and a half million between the years of 1830 and today. Of all the major waves of immigrants to the new world, they were the most diversified in background. There were farmers and intellectuals, artisans and tradesmen, Protestants, Catholics and Jews. They landed at all the leading harbors and settled in all sections of the United States.

The high tide of German immigration came as that from Ireland began to recede. When Americans of the mid-nineteenth century spoke of immigrants, they meant the Irish and the Germans. The very real contrasts in national character between the two were exaggerated by writers of several generations to gain dramatic and comic effects. For years, vaudeville teams got their best laughs by pitting Paddy, the temperamental stage Irishman, against the German stereotype, the good-natured, patient "Dutchman" with his red nose and tipsy gait, a glass of beer in his hand and a string of sausages dangling from his arm.

The older American thought the German thrifty and industrious, and admired many of his qualities. Yet the German was not always welcomed, nor did he always make a compatible neighbor.

At the beginning of the nineteenth century, the map of Europe showed no nation named Germany; the German speaking population was subdivided into thirty-eight separate states. Each state had its own flag, its own laws and constitution, its own king or duke, jealous of his power. Every ruler had an army, ready to crush all opposition.

In contrast to this somber picture, the German states were also the home of several outstanding universities; around them clustered some of the most advanced thinkers of that era. Philosophers and journalists, students and professors gathered in secret meetings to discuss the future of their country. They wanted social and political reforms, personal freedom for their people, a unified country, which would not be subject to the whims of three dozen petty rulers. Since none of the rulers were willing to give up their power, several rebellions took place and were ruthlessly suppressed.

In Frankfurt, a large group of intellectuals met in 1848 to try to compose a constitution that would unify the country. For weeks they planned and debated, but their differences were too deep for compromise. The Parliament ended in failure, and revolt and repression followed once more. Many of the rebels were locked up in jail, some went into hiding. Most of them fled the country and eventually crossed the ocean to America. These few thousand brave men, who later came to be known as the Forty-Eighters, were to provide the initial leadership for the growing German-American community in the United States.

Most of the people in the German states who came to American had no concern with politics or revolution. If they lived on the land, as the major part of them did, wars and rumors of wars, crop failures and population growth made for poverty and restlessness. When they heard of forty-acre farms available in America for eight to twelve dollars an acre, the farmers' discontent found a positive outlet.

Agents from America were most active in the German states. Real estate promoters and representatives of western states and territories advertised heavily for settlers. Shipping companies passed around handbills and posted schedules of sailings on the walls at street corners. The farmers were not alone in taking notice.

Artisans and mechanics also felt the shock waves of political unrest and rural poverty. Trained in the master system, where one man learned to make an entire article, these craftsmen were also being threatened by the rise of factories, which could be manned by unskilled labor. Across the ocean, an expanding America was eager for skilled men.

Going to America became a cure for all ills, whether po-

German immigrants for New York embarking on a Hamburg steamer.
Minnesota Historical Society.

German immigrants at Castle Garden in New York City
from *Harper's Weekly*, April, 1871.

litical, social or economic. The emigration craze swept through the German states from Bavaria to Prussia, as though people wanted to disprove their reputation for patience and solidity, for love of home and land.

According to a newspaper of the day:

"One night the thought entered the mind of the house-holder that emigration might be a desirable step; the next day he talked it over with his friends and each strengthened the resolution of the other; on the morning of the third day they all engaged passage."

It may have taken somewhat more than three days to reach the decision to forsake the cottage or the farm that had been home for untold generations. Yet make it they did, in such numbers that at times entire villages were left deserted.

In the great majority of cases, the head of the family managed to sell his possessions before he left; he started on his journey with a small amount of capital to help him begin life across the ocean. There were a few who emigrated as pau-pers, their voyage paid by the township where they lived. But among German emigrants, they were in the minority.

The German states varied in their attitude toward this *Volkerwanderung*, this mass exodus of people. For the most part they did not resist it, except in the case of young men up for military service. Even for these, it was not too difficult to slip over the border into France or Switzerland, and from there make their way to a harbor.

The German states were probably the first in Europe to try to protect their subjects from the many dangers of the journey. Laws were passed regulating the sale of ocean pas-sages and the building of good train connections. Booths were set up at railroad stations, at river docks and market places, where a bewildered peasant from the interior could get a list of rooming houses or the sailing dates of ships. At Bremen, a special lodging house was erected. It served as a model for port towns throughout Europe.

The harbors of Hamburg and Bremen competed with each other for the immigrant trade. Ships left these towns on regular schedules bound for America, and returned loaded with tobacco and other staples. On the days preceding the sailings—usually the first and fifteenth of each month—the streets of both cities bustled with human traffic; in forty-eight hours the travelers would be gone, soon to be replaced by a new crowd.

The middle of the nineteenth century saw a number of improvements in transatlantic travel. In 1855, Great Britain and the United States both passed laws attempting to regulate shipboard conditions. In the same year, New York City opened a new immigrant landing depot at Castle Garden, thereby putting an end to at least some of the perils that had awaited voyagers on arrival. Gradually, sailing vessels were replaced by steamships; the voyage then took two weeks rather than six or eight, and prices were far lower.

Boatloads of German immigrants landed in New York, in Philadelphia, and New Orleans. As early as 1847 a society was formed to help the immigrants and to keep alive among them a feeling for the German language and traditions. The National Society for German Emigrants printed maps and guidebooks, and made available up-to-date information on land and economic opportunities. A man could go from city to city in the new world receiving advice from branches of the organization.

Important German settlements arose in New York State, and in the South; Pennsylvania appealed to great numbers of newcomers who knew that German communities had flourished there since colonial days. The greatest majority of German immigrants, however, headed West, if not to the actual frontier, then to the territory just behind it.

German farmers enjoyed a good reputation in the United States; many states offered special concessions to induce them to settle. With typical thoroughness, groups of farmers would select their area carefully, often sending ahead a scout to look over what was available. They preferred wooded land, which, after clearing, offered the finest soil; they made certain they would be close to market towns. Frequently a German would buy a farm that had been partially cleared by an American pioneer ready to move on.

In Ohio and Missouri, Indiana, Illinois and especially in Wisconsin, the German found his ideal location. He proceeded to fertilize the soil, diversify his crops, and remove the tree stumps that the less thorough Yankee had left in the fields. With his first earnings he bought a few cows and a bull and went into dairy and livestock farming as a sideline. Many farmers, remembering the vine covered banks of the Rhine, planted a few grape arbors and made their own wine.

The whole family helped with the outside work; it was to the land itself that their efforts were devoted, not to the home. A German farmer in Missouri wrote home to describe the 150 acres he had bought for $1,000. He had planted corn, wheat, oats, potatoes, cotton and pumpkins, he said. He owned a number of plows, harnesses and various implements. He was raising chickens, bees, hogs, cattle, sheep and horses. And then, as an afterthought, he added,

"I have just finished a house, which cost me $45."

To the American farmer, the German seemed a penny pincher. But the feeling of disapproval was quite mutual. The German farmer considered the American wasteful and frivolous; frowned on his hobby of whittling and on his rude habits. Another Missouri German expressed this feeling in a letter to his relatives:

"There is scarcely a farm that is not for sale, for the American farmer has no love for home, such as the German has."

The German bought his land for keeps, intending to pass it on to his children and grandchildren, as in the old country. In this manner he developed more than 672,000 farms.

The Western states that appealed to the farmer were usually the same ones selected by the artisans and tradesmen, who
moved into the nearby cities. Chicago; Cincinnati and Cleveland in Ohio; St. Louis, Missouri; and Milwaukee, Wisconsin
became important German centers after the middle of the
nineteenth century. In these growing cities the new arrivals
from Germany formed their own separate communities,
where the customs and traditions of their former lives were
carried out in every possible detail.

Frederika Bremer, a Swedish writer, who published a
diary of her American travels in the 1850s, described several
of these cities:

"The Germans live here," Miss Bremer wrote of
Cincinnati, "as in their old Germany. They are *gemütlich,*
drink beer, practise music . . ."

Of Milwaukee, the traveler reported:

"Nearly half of the inhabitants are German, and they oc-
cupy a portion of the city to themselves, which is called 'German Town'. This lies on the other side of the river Milwaukee.
Here one sees German houses, German inscriptions over the
doors or signs, German physiognomies. Here are published
German newspapers, and many Germans live here who never
learn English and seldom go beyond German Town. The Germans in the Western states seem for the most to band together
in a clan-like manner, to live together and amuse themselves
as in their fatherland. Their music and dances, and other popular pleasures, distinguish them from the Anglo-American
people, who, particularly in the West, have no other pleasure
than business."

This last remark was one that found wide response
among German immigrants. Tradesmen, artisans or farmers,
all found ample opportunity for their talents in the expanding
atmosphere of nineteenth century America. Economic improvement was readily available. But they did not find the opportunities for relaxation that they had enjoyed in the old

country. American food they considered unpalatable; they deplored the lack of music in the daily lives of most people; and certainly nobody in the new world knew how to make proper beer. They missed the old *gemütlichkeit,* the cozy, cheerful quality of their old life. And they wasted no time in developing it in their communities.

They formed their own singing societies, opened their own cafes and restaurants, arranged frequent picnics and dances. Most influential among the organizations started were the *Turnvereine.* These athletic clubs had originated in Europe and emphasized both physical and mental progress. By 1860 there were branches in all the major cities of the United States, and it was their influence that resulted in the introduction of physical education in American public schools, and in the founding of the YMCAs.

On Sunday the *Turnvereine* and other clubs held concerts for their members. After the concert the whole family would go to a beer garden to eat and listen to the music of a German band.

Native Americans, brought up on the tradition of the Puritan Sabbath, with church services the only allowed activity, disapproved of the Continental Sunday. They frowned on beer gardens and dancing and pleasure-seeking in general; as a result in the early days of German immigration great friction developed between the two groups.

Oddly enough, the conflict was aggravated by the very men who were the most outstanding among the newcomers: the refugees of the various German revolutions.

After each abortive rebellion in the German states a number of political exiles came to America. They worked, initially, at whatever job they could get, whether they were suited for it or not. There were college graduates building the Schuylkill Canal after the uprisings of 1831, and farmers cutting corn in Missouri with swords that had seen service in the Napoleonic wars. There were agricultural communities in Il-

St. Paul Turnverein, 1875. Minnesota Historical Society.

Musical group of the 1860's—from ambrotype.
Minnesota Historical Society.

linois, Wisconsin and Texas where the farmers recited Greek and Latin as they worked. "Latin Farmers," they were called, with mingled respect and sarcasm.

In such a settlement, a visitor was likely to see "a bookcase half filled with classics, half with sweet potatoes." He might be offered "coffee in tin cups upon Dresden saucers," and to be invited to sit on a barrel "to hear one of Beethoven's symphonies performed on a grand piano."

Many a Latin Farmer paid more attention to his books than to his sweet potatoes and went broke in the process. Most avoided bankruptcy by moving to the cities and entering the professions for which they had been trained.

The majority of political refugees came after the revolution of 1848. When they were forced to flee, they transferred their reforming zeal to the United States. In education and social standing, in personal bravery and political idealism, they had been leaders among their fellow citizens in the German states. In their new country not only were they leaders among their own people, but they advocated changes in the entire country. They were deeply opposed to the Puritan ideals which still prevailed in the 1850s. They found our politics rowdy and violent; and the very idea of slavery was repugnant to them. The Puritan Sunday, prayers and Bible readings in public schools they regarded an invasion of personal freedom. The reality of nineteenth century America, they discovered, was far short of the legend that had reached them in Europe.

Some of the Forty-Eighters, homesick and disappointed, returned to Europe to plot anew for the overthrow of tyranny. Some of those who remained here felt that the Germans had nothing to gain by becoming Americanized; they proposed a "New Germany," a wholly separate state to be created in Wisconsin. Not all of them went to such extremes. Many became editors of German language newspapers and used their columns as a springboard to further their favorite causes.

Certainly some of their criticism was justified. Much of it, however, was tactlessly stated. It angered many Americans and was used as ammunition by the nativist movement that was gathering strength throughout the country.

The collection of secret societies that merged into the Know-Nothing party had two guiding principles: anti-Catholicism and anti-foreignism. In some cities, it was the Irish Catholics who were considered the threat; in others, it was the Germans. They were the infidels, the radicals, the pleasure-seekers who wanted, "to bring in upon us the wretched immoralities of European society."

On many occasions, German parades, picnics and balls were disrupted by gangs of thugs and ended in riots. During the elections of 1855, there were disturbances in several cities; in the German section of Louisville, twenty people were killed.

The slavery issue, so divisive among nineteenth century Americans, became one of the great unifying forces in the German-American community. Farmers, craftsmen and mechanics were against slavery because they felt it kept farm prices and labor wages down. For the Forty-Eighters, abolition was a great moral cause, one to which they gladly devoted their reforming zeal. It was the initial reason for their involvement in American politics.

Carl Schurz, most prominent of the Forty-Eighters, wrote upon arrival in the United States:

"The slavery question, with all its social, political and economic bearings, stirred me at once, and deeply. I could not resist the desire to go to Washington and witness the struggle in Congress."

Schurz landed in New York in 1852, a recent bridegroom in his mid-twenties with a red beard and a reputation for derring-do. As a student he had been imprisoned for his part in the revolution of 1848. He had fled to Switzerland through a sewer line leading to the river Rhine. From there, not content with his own safety, he had once more crossed the frontier to free his friend and former professor, Gottfried Kinkel.

Once in America, Schurz plunged into the political life of the country. Not for him the separatist notions of some of his fellow-reformers.

"We as Germans are not called upon here to form a separate nationality," Carl Schurz once said, "but rather to contribute to the American nationality the strongest there is in us, and in place of our weakness to substitute the strength wherein our fellow Americans excel us, and blend it with our wisdom . . . We should never forget that in the political life of this republic, we as Germans have no peculiar interests, but that the universal well-being is ours also."

Settling in Watertown, Wisconsin, Schurz taught himself the English language with amazing rapidity.

"I did not use an English grammar," he reminisced many years later. "I do not think I ever had one in my library. I resolutely began to read . . . first my daily newspaper . . . then I proceeded to read English novels . . . Shakespeare's plays came last . . . I never permitted myself to skip a word . . . and I never failed to consult the dictionary in every doubtful case."

His talents were soon recognized by the men organizing the new Republican party, and before long Schurz was much in demand as a speaker in the German-American community. In 1859, he delivered a speech in Boston's Faneuil Hall that helped defeat a bill designed to restrict the rights of the foreign born.

Against the idea that newcomers cannot be trusted to know how to vote, he said, "The noble doctrine that liberty is the best school for liberty and that self-government cannot be learned but by practicing it. This, sir, is a truly American idea; this is true Americanism, and to this I pay the tribute of my devotion."

Carl Schurz

The speech was widely read and came to the attention of Senator Abraham Lincoln. The two men became friends; Schurz barnstormed the country campaigning for Lincoln during the Presidential election of 1860. It was the start of a long and varied career of service to his adopted country.

Lincoln appointed Schurz minister to Spain. He returned to America at the start of the Civil War to serve as a general. After the war, he moved to St. Louis. Sixteen years after his arrival in the United States, he was elected senator from Missouri. During the administration of President Hayes, he served with great distinction as Secretary of the Interior.

Throughout his years in public life, he pioneered causes that only much later caught the nation's interest. As Secretary of the Interior, he introduced the civil service system into his department and raised his voice against the treatment accorded the American Indian. One hundred years before conservation became a household word, he urged the preservation of public lands and the protection of forests.

Like Schurz, all the Forty-Eighters were devoted to the cause of the Civil War. If they were not serving as officers in the army, they were writing articles and addressing meetings, urging people to join up.

The German community responded with enthusiasm, for personal as well as patriotic reasons; land and bounties were offered as an incentive to enlist, and the government had promised to waive citizenship requirements for soldiers honorably discharged.

Long-time Americans who had questioned the loyalty of the foreign born were silenced by the high proportion of immigrants who volunteered. Still, there was much controversy over the use of "foreign troops," and German officers like Schurz and General Franz Sigel were accused of cowardice if the battle did not go their way.

The end of the Civil War saw great well being in the German-American communities and a renewed influx of arrivals from the homeland. The wave of German immigration reached its peak in the years between 1880 and 1890: a million and a half people in ten years. Success stories of Germans in America were widely publicized at home; while in this country, the German communities and their newspaper editors took great pride in the achievements of the German Empire. For Germany by then was a united country, united not under the idealistic principles of the Forty-Eighters but under the blood and iron rule of Prime Minister Bismark.

In the 1880s the days of free homesteads in the West were drawing to a close. The new immigrants from Germany were artisans and industrial workers rather than farmers, and they sought work in the factories and shops of the major cities. The German communities became larger and more tightly knit than ever, and the language spoken grew into a colorful mixture of the two idioms, dotted with phrases like:

"Die cow hat über die fence geyumpt."

The skill and efficiency of German workers were greatly appreciated by other Americans, even though their clannishness was often deplored. In those days, job openings often specified the desired nationality; the words "German preferred" appeared with great frequency.

In all the major cities, bakers and butchers were usually German, introducing into America's households such words as sauerkraut, pumpernickel, delicatessen, pretzel, and frankfurter and hamburger, both named after German cities. Beer, which had been virtually unknown in the United States before the middle of the nineteenth century, was a staple in German-American homes, and the making of several large fortunes.

There was also a concern for music and education. A lady from Galveston, Texas, described the influence of the Germans in music in the late 1800s as follows: "German male choruses came from all over the state to compete for prizes. Competition was keen, and the *Sängerfeste*—everybody used the word—were outstanding musical events; everybody went.

As a little girl I was fascinated by the many fat, tubby middle-aged Germans among the singers getting red and purple in the face while singing, particularly the tenors.

"German homes had amateur musical evenings, men, women and children contributing. It was a privilege to be invited. Something musical sponsored by Germans was always cropping up. Nearly all the music teachers in town were German."

The German school system was highly regarded by American educators of the late nineteenth century. When a German-American community established its own private school, it would draw a good many pupils from other families as well. Those German-American parents who chose to send their children to public schools made sure that German was taught, and taught well. In most states, this was so until the outbreak of World War I.

The most lasting of the many German contributions to our educational system is the kindergarten, which has retained its original name, meaning children's garden. It was Mrs. Carl Schurz who organized the first American kindergarten in Watertown, Wisconsin, in 1855. By the 1880s there were some five hundred play schools in the United States, many of them in slum areas, where they were needed to care for the children of working mothers.

But by the start of the twentieth century many of the young people were beginning to turn away from the German-oriented way of life of the communities.

"Soon they will close our German theaters and Turner halls," complains one of the characters in *Bucket Boy*, Ernest L. Meyer's memoir of a Milwaukee boyhood. "And all because we let our young people go to the nickel shows just to see one funny fellow hit another funny fellow with a pie in the face. Pfui!"

The normal process of Americanization was already at work, when the coming of World War I added its impact.

German infant school, 1867, as photographed by H. J. Jacoby.
Minnesota Historical Society.

Carnival of Nations, in Minnesota, January 1885.
Minnesota Historical Society.

For the first three years of the war, from 1914 to 1917, the United States was officially neutral in the conflict, which pitted Germany and Austria against Great Britain, France and Russia. In August 1914, President Wilson exhorted the nation to be "neutral in fact as well as in name . . . impartial in thought as well as in action."

In reality, the situation in this country was quite different. On the East and West coasts and in the South, many people and a large segment of the press took the side of the Allies from the very beginning. In the heart of the country, most Americans felt removed from the conflict, and wanted to remain that way. "I Didn't Raise My Boy to Be a Soldier" was one of the most popular songs of that era.

German-Americans were mostly neutralists, too, from lack of any real choice. They knew that if the United States went to war it would be on the side of Britain and France. But "impartial in thought"? Impartiality comes hard to people who have roots in a country at war. Relief funds were raised in large amounts in all German-American communities. People worried about their relatives and friends across the sea, and the German-language press went to great lengths to offset the pro-Allies attitude of many American newspapers.

Then, in April of 1917, President Wilson declared war against Germany.

"We have no quarrel with the German people," he said in a sorrowful speech. "We have no feeling towards them but one of sympathy and friendship."

It was, he explained, the belligerent attitude of the German Empire that was a threat to world peace. The President's tolerant attitude was not reflected by the people of his country. Overnight, everything German became suspect in the United States.

German music was dropped from concert and opera programs. Church services could no longer be held in German.

Throughout the country, the teaching of this once-popular language was dropped from school and college curriculums. In Columbus, Ohio, the school board sold its German books to a waste paper company, at fifty cents for each hundred pounds. In other cities books by German authors were pulled off the shelves of libraries and schools and publicly burned while town officials stood at attention and the town band played patriotic songs.

There were people who disapproved of this hysteria, but for the superpatriots, and for bitter, frustrated people in all walks of life, it was a heyday. For millions of Americans of German descent it was a time of persecution and tragedy. People who had been considered reliable, hard-working Americans, who had been good neighbors and friends, abruptly became the enemy.

The responsibility lay in part with the administration itself. In an attempt to turn the United States away from its neutralist attitude, the government launched a nationwide campaign to inspire support for the war. Pamphlets and editorials, speeches and motion pictures whipped up hatred for the enemy, the barbarous Hun. With the passage of the Espionage Act of 1917 and the Sedition Act of 1918, a wave of spy hunting spread over the land.

Security leagues and loyalty leagues sprung up in many communities for the purpose of reporting "suspicious" people and incidents. Anyone speaking German was reported to the police. People were brought to trial and convicted for making disloyal remarks about the Red Cross. German-Americans were publicly taunted and flogged and forced to kiss the American flag. Every German organization was seen as part of a conspiracy on the part of the German emperor, the evil Kaiser. Congress conducted an extensive investigation of the National German-American Alliance. It was found to be free of un-American motives, but the times were such that it dissolved anyway.

It was a time of great name-changing for German-sounding people and things. The town of Berlin, Iowa, was renamed Lincoln; Müller became Miller; Schmitt changed to Smith. Restaurants stopped serving sauerkraut and hamburger, offering "liberty cabbage" and "Salisbury steak" instead. The little dachshund became a fierce sounding "liberty hound."

There are aspects of this curious crusade that seem ridiculous today, but to the people involved the agony was very real. Many families were bitterly divided, some siding with the homeland, some with the United States. An exchange of letters between two feuding brothers was considered important enough in 1917 to be published by a leading magazine. Rudolf Heinrichs, writing to his pro-German brother Felix, bitterly questioned the wisdom of their Germanic upbringing.

"The basic principle by which the American people has grown great has been brought into question by the German-Americans. Are we merely an agglomeration of Euopean expatriates?" he asks his brother, and himself, "or are we a new people, richer in promise, as we believe, than any race which has yet existed?"

The overwhelming majority of German-Americans believed they were indeed a new people, and cast their lot with their adopted country.

"Even as a man leaves his father and mother and bestows his affection upon his wife, so have we done in the matter of country," was the way one newspaper expressed the feeling of most people of German descent. Thousands of young men served in the American Expeditionary Force, under the command of General John J. Pershing, who was himself descended from a German family.

By the end of the war, the hysteria against German-Americans had spent itself. After a time, German was taught again in schools, though not as widely as before; and German music was again granted its rightful place. Yet time and the war had left their mark; the German-American community never regained that cohesiveness it had held for half a century.

Several decades later, when the German nation was in the grip of the Nazi movement, most Americans of German descent kept aloof from identification with the homeland.

There was, for a time, a German-American Bund, an organization that was openly pro-Nazi. With their black boots and swastika armbands, their Nazi flag and anti-Semitic slogans, they held noisy rallies and made violent speeches. But they never drew more than a negligible minority of the population. When the United States entered World War II in 1941, the whole movement collapsed.

At the opposite end of the political spectrum were those German-Americans who openly denounced Adolf Hitler and his ideals. Their feelings were expressed by Wendell Willkie, author of *One World*. Willkie had been defeated by Franklin Delano Roosevelt in his bid for the Presidency, but had become a firm supporter of the President's foreign policy. In February of 1941 Willkie made an official visit to the embattled city of London and spoke by shortwave to the people of Germany.

"I am of purely German descent. My grandparents left Germany ninety years ago because they were protestants against autocracy and demanded the right to live as free men. I, too, claim that right. I am proud of my German blood. But I hate aggression and tyranny. And my convictions are shared to the full by the overwhelming majority of my fellow countrymen of German descent. . . . We German-Americans reject and hate the aggression and lust for power of the present German government."

For most German-Americans at the time of the Second World War, there was no longer a problem of divided loyalties. They had been American citizens for several generations. The ties to the old country were gone.

As a consequence of the war and of Nazi persecutions, a new wave of refugees from Germany came to America's shores. Their story will be told in a later chapter.

"America Fever" Sweeps Scandinavia

O N O C T O B E R 15, 1825, an article appeared in one of New York's leading newspapers, the *Daily Advertiser*, entitled "A Novel Sight."

"A vessel has arrived at this port with emigrants from Norway," the reporter wrote. "The vessel is very small, measuring only about 360 Norwegian lasts, or 45 American tons, and brought 46 passengers, male and female, all bound to Ontario County, where an agent, who came over some time since, purchased a tract of land.

"The appearance of such a party of strangers coming from so distant a country and in a vessel of such size . . . could not but excite an unusual degree of interest. They have had a voyage of fourteen weeks; and all are in good health.

"An enterprise like this argues a great deal of boldness in the master of the vessel, as well as an adventurous spirit in the passengers . . .

"Those who came from the farms are dressed in coarse cloths of domestic manufacture, of a fashion different from the American; but those who inhabited the towns wear calicoes, ginghams and gay shawls, imported, we presume, from England.

"The vessel is built . . . with a single mast and top sail, sloop rigged. She passed through the English Channel and as far south as Madeira, where she stopped three or four days and then steered directly for New York, where she arrived with the addition of one passenger, born on the way."

In 1825, this was a "novel sight." Twenty-five years later, the sight of a Scandinavian sloop docking in an American harbor would be an everyday occurrence, one that would no longer "excite an unusual degree of interest." By mid-century, the people of Norway and Sweden, and, to a lesser degree, Denmark and Finland, were smitten with "America Fever."

More than one million Swedes came to the United States, one out of every six inhabitants of that country, and over one million more among Norwegians, Danes and Finns. Most of them made their move between 1840 and 1880.

It seemed at the time as though everyone in Scandinavia wanted to go to America. In fact, it was everyone who was tired of battling with poverty: of going out onto an icy sea, day after day, to bring home a meager catch of fish; of trying to wrench a living from a tiny plot of rocky land. The primary reason the Scandinavians left home was economic.

There was little religious oppression in the Northern countries, and a man was about as free there as he was anywhere in Europe at the time. The seeds of representative government had been planted, the beginnings of a public education system were in force. There was almost no illiteracy, especially among the younger people, the ones most anxious to emigrate.

It was the forces of nature that were the enemy: the short growing seasons and the scarcity of land. Then several years of crop failure came along, causing even greater hardships on small landowners and on the cotters who leased their farms. Whole families left together, often groups of related families. At times a small village would be left empty.

The ruling classes of Norway and Sweden worried for fear they would lose all their working people; they tried to stop the movement, but to no avail. Newspapers ran articles denouncing the myth of a golden America, clergymen thundered from the pulpit that the United States was a godless land; but the America Fever raged on, became an epidemic. The vision of a homestead in the new land was not to be denied.

It was largely the "America letters" that spurred this great migration across the sea, hundreds of letters from friends and neighbors who had gone first and wrote home to tell about it.

In those days, receiving a letter was a rare thing. Letters from across the sea, were, it was said, "borne in triumph, and opened with joy." When a letter from America arrived in a remote, pine clad village in Scandinavia, it would be read not merely by the family for whom it was meant, but by everyone for miles around.

The letters spoke of everyday things, for they were written by former neighbors, who knew what would interest the folks at home. They told of the cost of land, of work available and the wages one could earn, of the number of cows a man might own, the free public schools his children could attend. They spoke of sickness and hardship, too, but that only made it more real to the impoverished farmers and fishermen who read the letters.

In wonder, the village people would listen to the words of the traveler describing this promised land.

"The American treats his employees well," one letter read, "he does not treat them as servants but as helpers. He expects good work, it is true, but then wages, food and treatment are as fine as you can wish."

Another read, "Here, it is not asked, what or who was your father, but the question is, what are you?"

Or, "I have proof that it must be good to live here: it is only five years ago that people began to cultivate the land and now there are some who have already become wealthy."

And then the writer added: "If you would show this letter to Mr. Bagger, you might ask him if he will have it printed in the Skien newspaper, so that others who have asked me to write may see it."

Many others did see it, and ponder it, and discuss it. Their interest whetted by the "America letters," they listened intently to the emigration agents sent from America.

These agents represented American railroad companies, anxious to sell tickets and also the land they owned along the railroad lines. Some of them represented the government of a state anxious to increase its population. Often these representatives were former immigrants, returning home in the employ of an American company.

People walked many miles when they heard that an American agent was in the neighborhood. They came to see him flash a gold watch, a purse filled with American money, the latest clothes worn in the country across the sea. At times the agent lied, exaggerating the opportunities he was supposed to represent. More often he served a useful role, answering questions and bringing information his listeners wanted to hear.

There was also a book the people of Scandinavia were reading. They called it simply *The America Book*, but it had been entitled *True Account of America for the Information and Help of Peasant and Commoner*. The author, Ole Rynning, unlike most of the people who pored over his small volume, was a well-educated young Norwegian, the son of a minister. In 1837, he had led a group of eighty-four farmers to America to build a settlement in Illinois.

The venture was plagued by bad luck and disease. Lying

EMIGRATION

UP THE MISSISSIPPI RIVER.

The attention of Emigrants and the Public generally, is called to the now rapidly improving

TERRITORY OF MINNESOTA,

Containing a population of 150,000, and goes into the Union as a State during the present year. According to an act of Congress passed last February, the State is munificently endowed with Lands for Public Schools and State Universities, also granting five per cent. on all sales of U. S. Lands for Internal Improvements. On the 3d March, 1857, grants of Land from Congress was made to the leading Trunk Railroads in Minnesota, so that in a short time the trip from New Orleans to any part of the State will be made in from two and a half to three days. The

CITY OF NININGER,

Situated on the Mississippi River, 35 miles below St. Paul, is now a prominent point for a large Commercial Town, being backed by an extensive Agricultural, Grazing and Farming Country; has fine streams in the interior, well adapted for Milling in all its branches; and Manufacturing **WATER POWER** to any extent.

Mr. JOHN NININGER, (a Gentleman of large means, ideas and liberality, speaking the various languages,) is the principal Proprietor of **Nininger**. He laid it out on such principles as to encourage all **MECHANICS**, Merchants, or Professions of all kinds, on the same equality and footing; the consequence is, the place has gone ahead with such rapidity that it is now an established City, and will annually double in population for years to come.

Persons arriving by Ship or otherwise, can be transferred without expense to Steamers going to Saint Louis; or stop at Cairo, and take Railroad to Dunleith (on the Mississippi). Steamboats leave Saint Louis and Dunleith daily for **NININGER**, and make the trip from Dunleith in 36 to 48 hours.

NOTICES.

1. All Railroads and Steamboats giving this card a conspicuous place, or *gratuitous insertion* in their cards, AIDS THE EMIGRANT, and forwards their own interest.

2. For authentic documents, reliable information, and all particulars in regard to Occupations, Wages, Preempting Lands in neighborhood, Lumber, Price of Lots, Expenses, &c., apply to

THOMAS B. WINSTON, 27 Camp street, **New Orleans.**
ROBERT CAMPBELL, St. Louis.
JOSEPH B. FORBES, Dunleith.

Handbill from Donnelly scrapbook: Immigration up the
Mississippi River. Minnesota Historical Society.

in a sick bed in a log hut, his feet frozen and bleeding, Rynning wrote his guide book in an attempt to help others avoid some of the errors his group had made.

He suggested the kinds of clothes and food that should be brought along for the journey. A fishing rod and tackle would be useful to have on board ship, he wrote, a good pipe for the husband, a spinning wheel for the lady. Medicines should be packed, and plenty of vinegar for washing down the cabin. He even gave advice on how to make a contract with the ship's captain as to how much water and wood he would provide at sea, and what kind of casks should hold the water. Make sure, he said, that the captain's drinking water comes from the same casks that supply his passengers.

He gave practical information about life in the United States, too, in brief, simple form. A fellow settler took the manuscript back to Scandinavia, where it was immediately published. Rynning himself never saw the book; he died in 1838, before his thirtieth birthday, of the same malaria that had infected the entire settlement.

The words of advice he left for his countrymen were read by thousands, and carefully heeded. Throughout the Scandinavian peninsula hopeful people prepared for their new life with characteristic thoroughness.

They would try to leave in early spring, so that, once across the ocean, they could quickly plant crops to tide them over their first winter.

"All through the winter darkness," a young girl wrote, "I helped my mother with the preparations. In the evening, my brother and I often sat and built air castles, dreaming of what we would do when we got to America."

The preparations began with the spinning of yarn, to be woven into cloth for new clothes. Then they would build chests —immigrant trunks, they came to be called—that would be crammed with supplies. They would slaughter cattle and prepare the meat so it would not spoil on the way, bake flatbread and fashion barrels in which to pack it.

As the day of departure grew near, they would plan an auction to sell all they could not take, and then set forth on the journey to the seaport.

This is how Hans Mattson, a prominent Swedish-American, remembered the scene:

"We put our little emigrant trunk in father's old cart, and with many tears and the breaking of tender heartstrings we bade farewell to our brothers and sisters. Mother went with us as far as the churchyard, so that she could say that she had followed us to the grave . . .

"When we were a little past the farm called Branslan, I turned to take a final look at our village, Norrback, and I felt as if my heart was being torn from my bosom. When we passed the dear old church, my soul was again stirred to its depth as I recalled that it was here that I had been baptized and confirmed and had taken part in the worship, and now I would most likely never see it again. . . ."

For some, reaching the seaport meant traveling on foot or by oxcart all the way to France or Germany, then perhaps by boat to England. As the tide of emigration swelled, Norwegian and Swedish ships were built in ever growing numbers, and the price of a ticket decreased gradually from $35, to $25, to $15.

While they walked the roads, or as they waited for the ship's approach, the immigrants tried to dispell some of their sadness and fear by singing. Some of their songs spoke of the reasons for leaving:

> Farewell Norway, and God bless thee.
> Stern and severe wert thou always, but
> As a mother I honor thee, even though
> Thou skimped my bread.

> Other lands offer me independence, a
> Decent return for my labor, well-being
> For my kin. These, O Norway, thou
> Didst not give me.

Other ballads pictured the sadness of traditions left behind:

> Farewell, my old spinning wheel, now
> I must leave you, and my heart is near
> Breaking in my breast.
> No longer shall we sit chatting, you
> And I, before the fire in the evening.

> Alas, all I see about me has roots deep
> In my heart. Do you wonder it bleeds
> When they are pulled up?

Of all the ballads and songs that remain, the most famous is entitled "Oleana."

"Oleana" was the nickname given to a settlement in Pennsylvania, originally named New Norway. It was a venture conceived by Ole Bull, a well-known Norwegian violinist and composer who visited the United States in 1843. For two years he toured the new world, giving concerts and composing music inspired by the prairie, by Niagara, by the city of Washington.

In 1852, Bull poured the earnings from his concerts into the purchase of 120,000 acres in Potter County, Pennsylvania.

He planned to found a communal settlement, patterned on several started by Scandinavian immigrant groups. Norwegians were stunned when they heard of his investment; articles and editorials doubted that any one man could own so much land. Actually, Bull had contracted for even more.

The violinist was very popular among his countrymen,

and they responded rapidly and in large numbers to his plans for a settlement. The first group of thirty colonists arrived in September of 1852. On September 7th and 8th, a dedication ceremony took place, at which Ole Bull spoke, establishing "a New Norway, consecrated to liberty, baptized with independence and protected by the Union's mighty flag."

Work started on clearing the land, and Bull himself took out American citizenship papers, to the horror of many eminent people back home. He made noble plans for his colony, including a great technical school, which he felt America needed.

The first signal that something was amiss was sounded by a Norwegian minister, the Reverend Jacob Aal Otteson, who stopped to preach at New Norway on his way to Wisconsin. In a letter home, he wrote: "I truly believe that Ole Bull means very well, but he is not a business man."

The minister was more prophetic than he knew. The famous violinist had been talked into buying land that was difficult to clear and cultivate, far from the nearest railroad. Worse still, some of the acreage to which he had been given title belonged to others. Ole Bull had been swindled.

There was little bitterness toward Ole Bull even among his settlers, and he tried to help them pay off their debts and find better land. Back home, a ballad was written that became popular on both sides of the ocean. It shows the high hopes of the emigrants as well as the scepticism of some of their countrymen.

> In Oleana, that's where I'd like to be,
> And not drag the chains of slavery in
> Norway.
> > Ole—Ole—Ole—Oh! Oleana!
> > Ole—Ole—Ole—Oh! Oleana!
> In Oleana they give you land for nothing,
> And the grain just pops out of the ground.

Golly, that's easy.
   Ole—Ole—Ole—Oh! Oleana!
   Ole—Ole—Ole—Oh! Oleana!
And the salmon, they leap like mad
In the rivers, and hop into the kettles,
And cry out for a cover.
   Ole—Ole—Ole—Oh! Oleana!
   Ole—Ole—Ole—Oh! Oleana!
And little roasted piggies rush about
The streets, politely inquiring if you
Wish for ham.
   Ole—Ole—Ole—Oh! Oleana!
   Ole—Ole—Ole—Oh! Oleana!

Within a year of the dedication ceremony, all of Ole Bull's colonists had left Pennsylvania and were heading westward, where land was fertile and available, and where most Scandinavians were settling.

It was the western prairies that held the strongest appeal for the Norwegians, the Swedes, the Danes and the Finns, and to reach their promised land, they underwent endless privations.

There are newspaper accounts of boatloads of Swedish families arriving in New York in the 1850s, marching in a body toward the railroad station laden with their trunks, and carrying two flags: that of Sweden and of the United States.

Often they would be met by a representative of one of the benevolent societies that helped newcomers get started. They would take the train to Buffalo, then a lake boat or a wagon to the upper valleys of the Mississippi River. Or else they might take a river boat up the Hudson as far as Albany, then follow the Erie Canal to Buffalo, from there take a boat across the Great Lakes and then go overland.

At the very least, the trip took four or five months. Trains, barges and boats were as overcrowded as the ships on

Wood engraving of a company of Swedish immigrants bound west.
Library of Congress.

Interior of immigrant train from *Harper's Weekly*.
Minnesota Historical Society.

which the immigrants crossed the ocean. Again, the newcomer provided his own food and water.

Often, a man would have spent all his money long before he reached his destination. There were people waiting to exploit him every step of the way. "Runners" would approach him, usually speaking his native tongue, and offer him rooms, tickets, opportunities that did not exist. If his funds did not hold out, he would have to work along the way to earn more.

The men in the family would hire themselves out as farmhands or construction gang workers to earn $1 a day or less. The young girls would become servants; the women would take in washing. When their funds were replenished, they would continue their journey.

Hans Mattson, who arrived from Sweden in 1851, describes in his autobiography what greeted the immigrant when he arrived at his chosen destination, in this case, Minnesota.

"Looking back to those days," he wrote, "I see the little cabin, often with a sod roof, single room used for domestic purposes, sometimes crowded almost to suffocation by hospitable entertainment to newcomers; or the poor immigrant on the levee at Red Wing, just landed from a steamer, in his short jacket and other outlandish costume, perhaps seated on a wooden box, with his wife and a large group of children around him, wondering how he shall be able to raise enough means to get himself ten or twenty miles into the country, or to redeem the bedding and other household goods which he has perchance left in Milwaukee as a pledge for his railroad and steamboat ticket . . ."

They were long on perseverance, the Scandinavian immigrants, deeply religious and physically hardy. Somehow they did earn enough money, redeem their household goods, cover the endless miles by wagon, or on foot, and finally reach that prairie homestead for which they so longed.

They followed the streams, so they would have water and

A dug-out on Yellowstone Valley Ranch in Minnesota.
Minnesota Historical Society.

wood available, and made their supplies stretch until they could raise their own food.

The sod houses in which they first lived were a single room, twelve feet long and fourteen feet wide. They were built up against a slope, with two or three steps down to the dirt floor. Daylight came in through the door, smoke went out through a hole in the sod roof. For chairs and tables, they used the trunks they had built back home. They made brooms from prairie grass, pillows from the down of cattails.

They lived through prairie fires and draughts, locusts that ravaged their newly planted crops, snowstorms so blinding that a man had to stretch a wire to guide him from his house to his barn. There were no schools or churches; the nearest market might be thirty miles away, or it might be a hundred. By oxcart, if you covered twenty miles in a day you were doing well. When sickness struck, and it often became an epidemic, there were no doctors available, only the old-fashioned remedies of immigrant wives.

These were the trials that all pioneers endured, be they newcomers or native-born. But for the immigrants, there was the additional burden of strangeness, isolation, inability to communicate.

"The sense of being lost in an alien culture," is the way Ole Rölvaag describes the feeling, "the sense of being thrust somewhere outside the charmed circle of life. If you couldn't conquer that feeling, if you couldn't break through the magic hedge of thorns, you were lost indeed."

Rölvaag was the author of *Giants in the Earth*, a novel of pioneer life. Himself a newcomer from Norway, he paints an unforgettable picture of the loneliness, homesickness and fears that hounded the immigrant pioneers. Some were completely overwhelmed by the prairie. Most of them fought back with strength and stubbornness, conquering the hostile environment.

Eventually the sod cabins gave way to log houses;

schools and churches were built. Scandinavian ministers preached in their native tongues and worried lest their flock lose touch with the old culture.

Thousands of settlements went up in Illinois, Wisconsin, Iowa, Michigan, Indiana, North and South Dakota, and especially in Minnesota.

In 1853, Frederika Bremer, a Swedish lady traveling in the United States, had written:

"What a glorious new Scandinavia might not Minnesota become! Here would the Swede find again his clear, romantic lakes, the plains of Scania rich in corn, and the valleys of Norrland; here would the Norwegian find his rapid rivers, his lofty mountains, for I include the Rocky Mountains and Oregon in the new kingdom; and both nations, their hunting fields and their fisheries. The Danes might here pasture their flocks and herds and lay out their farms on richer and less misty coasts than those of Denmark . . ."

Scandinavian immigrants agreed wholeheartedly with her description of Minnesota. Today, in that state, there are more than four hundred place names of Scandinavian origin. There is Linstrom and Strandquist, Malmo, Norseland and New Sweden.

Once the prairie was turned into a thriving farmland some of the immigrants, or in many cases their children, moved further west toward the Pacific Ocean. Many entered the logging industry, providing lumber for the homes of later pioneers. Others became skilled craftsmen, carpenters and contractors, and helped to build the new cities of the West Coast.

Within a relatively short time Scandinavian immigrants were active in every aspect of life in the United States. Their Americanization proceded very rapidly, for a number of reasons.

Language was not much of a problem; the Nordic tongues were first cousins to English. The fact that most of

Barn raising on the Rainy River in Minnesota about 1890.
Minnesota Historical Society.

I. Ellefson's early house in Hendricks, Minnesota about 1880.
Minnesota Historical Society.

them were literate on arrival made a second language much easier to master.

"The interesting fact was that a Swedish emigrant and his wife learned the language of the new country so well before the children began coming that four of the five children never learned Swedish and the one who did learned it outside the home."

That is how things were in the Illinois home of Carl Sandburg, well-loved American poet, son of a Swedish blacksmith.

Most Scandinavians came over in families, firmly intending to settle for good, therefore they identified from the start with the affairs of their adopted country. Because their homelands were not involved in major wars, they were not caught in the same painful conflict that beset other immigrant groups. They were free to devote their energies to the land they had chosen.

They came to the United States at a time when there was a need for new people, and moved to an area that was ripe for settlement; the older inhabitants received them well. Feeling welcome, there was no need for them to develop defensive attitudes.

Their enthusiasm for American ways also stimulated those who stayed at home. The progress of Norwegians, Swedes and Danes in the new world was influential in bringing about reforms that made the Scandinavian countries among the most enlightened in Europe.

Throughout our history, public education has been an important Americanizing influence; from the very first, the Scandinavians were devoted supporters of public schools. Education today owes a number of important developments to their influence; home economic classes in our junior and senior high schools were patterned on those of Scandinavia, as were courses in shop and crafts. 4-H Clubs were begun at a farm school in Minnesota.

Norwegian church and school in Hemingford, Nebraska, 1889.
Minnesota Historical Society.

When Scandinavian newcomers turned their attention to higher education, they found it in short supply in the states where they had settled. Swedish and Norwegian communities founded a number of small colleges, most of them under Lutheran sponsorship. Many are still in existence; St. Olaf College in Minnesota, for example, is famous for the fine choral group it sponsors, and for its emphasis on Scandinavian culture.

Assimilation proceded at such a pace that clergymen and community leaders became concerned; they bent every effort toward preserving the language and the culture of home. Christmas customs persisted, and a preference for traditional foods. But by the time new waves of immigrants started to arrive, Scandinavians were thought of as native Americans, and so considered themselves.

Years of Transition

THE SIZE OF THE IRISH, German and Scandinavian groups overshadowed several smaller migrations in the same period. People from Holland, France, Switzerland, Wales and other countries also crossed the Atlantic during the middle of the nineteenth century. Since all of them came from the Northern part of Europe, their stories are similar to those already told.

Toward the end of the century important changes began to occur in the nature of immigration to America. The year 1882 saw an unprecedented number of new arrivals: almost 800,000. Among them were more Germans and Scandinavians than ever before, but also, and for the first time, sizable numbers of people from Southern and Eastern Europe. From that time on, immigration from the North gradually decreased, while that from Southern and Eastern Europe began to climb to levels nobody had thought possible.

The industrial revolution, which had begun in England in the previous century, was spreading to less developed areas of the continent. In each country in turn, the changeover to factory production brought such radical shifts in living patterns that thousands of people were displaced from their occupations and were forced to look abroad for a livelihood. After enough people had gone, factory wages went up and brought gradual improvement in economic conditions; then, for the most part, workers were less eager to emigrate. This was the situation in the British Isles, in the German states, and in the countries of Scandinavia as the nineteenth century came to a close.

It was then that in Italy, Poland, Russia, among the varied peoples of the Austro-Hungarian Empire, in Greece, and in the Balkan countries, peasants and laborers were just beginning to feel the consequences of industrialization. At the same time, they started to hear about the golden land across the sea.

This did not happen by coincidence. The economy was booming in the United States. Thriving new industries were in constant search for cheap labor; if they found no response in one section of Europe, they sought another.

No sooner had a Greek or an Italian peasant, or an artisan in the Polish provinces, begun to think about the possibility of going abroad to work, than an agent for an American concern was in his village, offering advice and encouragement.

Shipping companies, too, stood to profit from this new source of steerage passengers. They readied the harbors of the Mediterranean Sea and built new steamships that could cross the Atlantic in ten days with safety, if not with actual comfort.

Improved train transportation abroad enabled agents of industries and shipping companies to travel even to remote provinces, singing the praises of life in the new world. In direct response to their enticements, millions of people left their homes for America.

In the United States, this shift in immigrant nationality brought about far reaching changes in public attitude.

Previous waves of newcomers from Ireland, Germany and Scandinavia gradually came to be known as "old" immigrants, and in retrospect began to seem highly desirable. Americans argued that the physical appearance of the old immigrants was at least similar to their own; the old languages were related to English, and besides, over the years the accents had become familiar. The "new" immigrants conversed in tongues that sounded totally alien; they were mostly black-haired, dark-complexioned, shorter in stature. In other words, they were different looking. And they came from countries untouched by democratic traditions, where education was a luxury for the very few. A high proportion were illiterate.

In the popular mind, the earlier immigrants and their offspring took on new glamor. And they, in turn, forgetting their own difficult beginnings, joined the still older Americans in wondering whether the latest "greenhorns" could ever become law-abiding citizens of the United States. The "Monday pioneers" looked down on people who arrived on Tuesday.

Finley Peter Dunne, American humorist of Irish descent, remarked on this development. In one of his columns, the legendary bartender, Mr. Dooley, comments in his inimitable brogue:

As a pilgrim father that missed the first boat, I must raise me claryon voice again' the invasion iv this fair land be th' paupers an' arnychists in Europe. Ye bet I must—because I'm here first . . . In thim days America was th' refuge iv th' oppressed in all th' wurruld . . . But as I tell ye, 'tis diff'rent now. 'Tis time we put our back again' th' open dure an' keep out th' savage horde.

Immigrants in pens at
Ellis Island on or near
Christmas, 1906.
Library of Congress.

Ellis Island, showing an immigration official and immigrants with
their baggage, 1907. Museum of the City of New York.

Without a doubt the newcomers presented this country with serious problems. First of all, they came in overwhelming numbers, as many as a million a year. A new reception center had to be built to process the multitudes who landed in New York harbor. For more than thirty years, an average of 5,000 people a day passed through the huge, central registry room on Ellis Island: more than twenty-three million between 1880 and 1920.

A high percentage of the new arrivals were illiterate and therefore slow in taking part in the political life of the country. Often penniless, they were unable to travel any farther than the already crowded cities where their ships first docked. Even then, Americans were worrying about their cities.

At the turn of the century, and during the beginning of the 1900s, many citizens were bewildered by the changes taking place in the nation. The rural population, which had always considered itself the "real America," was rapidly being outnumbered by the inhabitants of the growing cities; the cities themselves were victims of industrialization and unchecked growth.

Farmers were poor, yet they raised ample crops. Industry prospered, but labor problems abounded. Who, or what, was to blame? Searching for answers, many people focused on the strange cities, which appeared to breed poverty and crime. Was it not the immigrants who peopled the cities and therefore created the problems? If so, the answer was to keep them out.

Because it came at a time of fear and instability, the rapid rise in the tide of immigration coupled with the change in nationalities created in this country a climate of deep hostility. Gradually the government was persuaded to legislate not just the numbers but the kind of immigrants who should be allowed to enter.

Until the 1880s, the government of the United States had made no effort to regulate immigration.

On Thanksgiving day in 1795, President Washington had offered a prayer that God might "render this country more and more a safe and propitious asylum for the unfortunate of other countries."

Some years later, Thomas Jefferson had asked with emotion, "Shall oppressed humanity find no asylum on this globe?"

Until 1820 the government had not even tried to keep track of how many new people landed each year. After that time, for some sixty years, a count was kept, but it was left up to the individual states to set their own rules for settlement if they so wished.

In 1882, Congress for the first time placed immigration under the supervision of the federal government. It also passed the earliest law excluding certain types of persons considered undesirable: convicts, people with extreme mental deficiencies, and those unable to care for themselves.

To these regulations, which most Americans considered justified, other, more stringent laws were added throughout the 1880s, including a statute barring immigration from China, which will be detailed in a later chapter.

In 1897, legislation was proposed excluding all who could not read or write. President Cleveland vetoed the law, giving rise to a controversy that lasted twenty years and divided the country. The proponents of a literacy test saw the ability to read and write as a measure of a person's basic intelligence. Those opposed held that an illiterate had merely been denied the opportunity to learn. The issue was debated until 1917, when the statute was adopted against the expressed wishes of President Wilson.

The issue of a man's ability to learn was the focal point in the national debate over limiting immigration. By the end of the nineteenth century, most sound thinking Americans felt that the numbers of immigrants were exceeding the country's capacity to absorb them. In addition, there were millions who

Music cover from 1879. Library of Congress.

Illustration from *Leslie's* Magazine, 1889, showing the results of unrestricted immigration: a Yankee becoming a possible curiosity. Library of Congress.

argued that the latest arrivals were incapable of learning because they were of inferior stock and would therefore never become good citizens.

Not all who held this view were simple-minded, ignorant people. The theory of racial superiority, which recent history has amply disproved, was sincerely held by vast numbers of educated persons throughout the world in the early decades of the present century. It was believed that there were essential, inborn differences in character and potential between peoples of different origins.

People in the United States were labeled "contentious Irishmen," or "order-loving Germans." The Chinese were "born gamblers." The Italian was "gay, light-hearted, and, if his fur is not stroked the wrong way, inoffensive as a child." As for the Jews, "money is their God."

These caricature images, far from being the words of a bigot, are quotes from *How the Other Half Lives,* an influential book written in 1890 by Jacob Riis. Riis was a talented reporter and photographer, and his descriptions of life in the poor quarters of New York City led to the first efforts at slum clearance. Yet even he, a crusading reformer, fell into the prejudiced thinking of his time.

If one believes that social and cultural traits are inborn, then one must assume that they are not affected by change in the environment. Therefore, moving to a new country, acquiring a job and an education, living in decent surroundings, still would not make a man of inferior stock the equal of a native-born American.

Congress set up an expert commission to study the entire question of immigration. Its investigation took more than three years to complete, employed three hundred people, cost one million dollars, and published its findings in forty-two volumes.

Ignoring obvious evidence, the commission concluded that there was indeed a difference between the old and the new

Bohemian cigarmakers at work in tenement in New York City.
Museum of the City of New York.

Italian mother and her baby living on Jersey Street in
New York City about 1889. Photograph by Jacob A. Riis, The
Jacob A. Riis Collection, Museum of the City of New York.

Russian steelworkers in Homestead,
Pennsylvania, 1909. Lewis W. Hine,
George Eastman House Collection.

Albanian woman at Ellis Island.
Lewis W. Hine, George Eastman
House Collection.

Finnish stowaway at Ellis Island.
Lewis W. Hine, George Eastman
House Collection.

Czechoslovakian grandmother.
Lewis W. Hine, George Eastman
House Collection.

immigration. The "old" had apparently landed on these shores equipped with all the requisites for American citizenship. The "new" would never make it.

The myth of Nordic superiority was officially acknowledged by the government of the United States. The groundwork was thus laid for the most stringent and most discriminatory immigration law ever to be adopted by this country.

The National Origins Act of 1924 set a ceiling on the total number of people allowed to immigrate in any one year. It also established the so-called "quota system," which specified how many immigrants of each nationality were permitted entry. The number was determined by the national origins of people in our population in 1920; it was heavily weighted in favor of immigrants from Northern Europe. Great Britain, Ireland, Germany and the Scandinavian countries were allotted some 70 per cent of the numbers available. The nations of Southern and Eastern Europe had minimal quotas; most of Asia was excluded altogether.

In countries where quota numbers were few, and where many wanted to emigrate, long waiting lists formed over the years. Greece, for instance, was allotted only 307 places a year; even if a man had close relatives in this country, it took years before he was able to join them. If he had no family in the United States, there was no chance for him at all. Meanwhile, thousands of quota numbers were wasted in countries that had large shares and few people anxious to leave.

The accident of being born in one part of the world instead of another, for some forty years determined a man's ability to enter the land whose constitution proclaimed "all men are created equal."

This was the climate in the United States as millions who had recently arrived struggled to adjust to their new country.

More than five million were Italians; four million hailed from the Austro-Hungarian Empire; almost half a million were Greeks; over three million were Russians, both Christians and Jews. Armenians came, fleeing cruel persecution; Chinese and Japanese, Spaniards, Poles, Rumanians, Czechs and Finns came. Changing boundaries make it difficult to determine the exact numbers from each country. Every religion was represented, every nationality.

To tell the story of each group in detail would be impossible. The next three chapters will explore some aspects of the "new" immigration.

The Coming of the Italians

MENTION ITALY TODAY and faces brighten in recognition. Italy is a country hordes of Americans dream of visiting. It is the land of sunny skies and culture, of high fashion and buxom movie stars, of red wine and spaghetti.

At the turn of the century, when millions of Italians were coming to find work in the United States, "spaghetti-eater" was an insulting word, tossed angrily at the newcomer. Italy was then a struggling young nation, recently unified and unable to feed large numbers of its people. The ruling classes were famous for their culture and wealth; the peasantry was poor and largely illiterate.

Ancient Romans had called the boot-shaped peninsula "Italia," but for more than one thousand years Italy had been only a poetic term, a dream in the minds of those who strove for unification. From the fall of the Roman Empire in 476 A.D. until 1870, the peninsula was a checkerboard of different states with ever-shifting borders. Waves of conquerors came down from the Alps, landed from the sea. Independent city-states vied with each other for territory and power. When Rome was proclaimed capital of the new kingdom of Italy, the young country found itself heir to conflicting loyalties, to strong local patriotism and to dozens of dialects as strange to each other as a foreign tongue.

Throughout the peninsula, agriculture prevailed. Much of the land was mountainous, and the areas that could be farmed were inadequate to feed the population. Traditionally, Italian working men had to leave their farms to find seasonal employment elsewhere. Many had gone to France and Germany, or to North Africa, where hundreds of thousands helped to dig the Suez Canal. In the early eighteen-hundreds, the more adventurous crossed the ocean to South America; two million Italians went to Brazil, two million more labored to build the cities of Argentina. By the middle of the nineteenth century, Italy's workers began to look toward the United States.

Individual Italians had been drawn to the American experiment since its inception. In 1620, the colony of Virginia invited a group of Venetian artisans to start a glass blowing trade. In the following century, a Florentine, Filippo Mazzei, led a group of farmers to Charlottesville, Virginia, where they introduced the culture of vines and silkworms.

Mazzei was a liberal writer and intellectual, and as a farmer he had little success. But he became a devoted partisan of the American cause, and a close friend and advisor to Thomas Jefferson. In 1773, Mazzei wrote a number of articles on political philosophy that Jefferson translated into English. In one of them we find these words, later echoed in the Declaration of Independence:

Tutti gli uomini sono per natura egualmente liberi e indipendenti. "All men are by nature equally free and independent."

Between the time of the Revolution and the Civil War, few Italians resided in the United States, although chronicles of the day do mention Italian street musicians in the larger cities, and vendors of plaster statuettes. There were political exiles, too, men who had sparked the many uprisings that finally brought about Italian unity. Even Giuseppe Garibaldi, one of Italy's founding fathers, sought temporary refuge on this continent; for some time he worked in a candle factory on Staten Island, in New York.

Italian sculptors, artists, and musicians had lent their talents to our new cities. Constantino Brumidi painted the frescoes in Washington's Capitol building, and Lorenzo da Ponte brought the first opera troupe to New York City.

After the 1850s, farmers and artisans began to cross the ocean in increasing numbers. They planted vineyards in New York State, and truck gardens on the outskirts of many large cities. Many followed the pioneers to California, where economic growth was just beginning. There they created the wine and fishing industries and met with ready success.

Most of them were people of comfortable means, from the more prosperous Northern Italy. They could afford to select the area where they wished to settle. Tales of their good fortune went back across the sea and gradually made their way to the poorer villages of the Italian south.

In crowded farmhouses, or sitting at lunch in the shade of a tree, men argued over what they would do once summer's harvest had been gathered. Many still talked of working in a mine across the Alps. But for more than five million Italian laborers, the lure of America was too strong to resist.

There were several immediate reasons for the mass flight from Italy. A sharp increase in population brought added hardship to an already overcrowded land. Then came a series of droughts, an economic crisis, and, in 1887, an epidemic of cholera. In Southern Italy there was no margin for additional disasters; everyday life was arduous enough.

In most communities the land belonged to a titled family who lived elsewhere. They owned the entire village, as in feudal days; the peasant family rented a piece of land, or else was paid a miserable daily wage. A foreman was engaged to make sure the peasant did his work; more often than not, he took advantage of both landlord and laborer.

There were few tools, no fertilizers, very little water. Women walked miles with huge jugs on their heads to stand in line before a village fountain. Even during the best of years it was difficult to earn enough to feed the entire family.

Sometimes there was a school some miles away, but it was mostly for the sons of the "signori," the gentry. A little barefoot peasant would not be welcomed by the child of the doctor or the lawyer. Besides, he was needed at home to tend the goats and sheep, to pull the plow, to gather grapes. And for this work, there was no need of learning.

"At eight or nine years of age, if not sooner, the peasant child is old enough to bend his neck to the yoke and to fix his eyes upon the soil . . .

"I remember labor, unremitting toil, exalted in the home, in the church, in the school, and its necessity quickly realized by the growing child . . ."

This was childhood, recalled by Angelo Pellegrini in his book, *Immigrant's Return.*

Men and boys, mothers and daughters all worked in the fields. Grandmothers minded the babies, spun yarn, and wove the clothes for the families' needs.

Several generations usually lived together in one room; the animals slept in the kitchen. The oldest male member of the family was in charge; each person had his role and duty, each family and village its traditions, unchanged for generations. A man most often lived and died in one house; for centuries his family had belonged to the same village.

In addition to work and family, the church played a central role in the life of the village. Mass on Sunday morning was an important event, attended by all the women and a scattering of men. Each village had a patron saint who looked after the people; it was to the saint's image that they brought their problems and their joys. The saint's special day was celebrated with a yearly holiday, which included music and parades as well as prayer.

Village in Italian is *paese*. A *paesano* is a man from one's own village. When necessity forced the Italian man to leave his village, he sought the advice of a *paesano* who had been abroad, and once across the sea he went to work with his own people, and lived as close to them as he could. In America, the *paesano* became a substitute for the family most men left behind.

The Italian laborer did not plan to remain in America; he meant to work perhaps a year or two, save his earnings, and go back to realize his dream: his own home, a bit of land, perhaps a pig or two. He wanted to return to the olive trees his great-grandfathers had planted, the orange and the lemon trees he had so carefully cultivated.

He left behind the women and the children to work the land in his absence. He hired out as part of a group to an American company, which prepaid his passage and guaranteed him work upon arrival.

So often were the immigrants of that time exploited and swindled, that in 1885 the American government passed a law forbidding contract labor from entering the country. From then on, all newcomers were asked to swear that they were not under contract to an employer. If they were, they were shipped back to their port of embarkation. In practice, the law changed things but little. The immigrant said he had no contract, but in fact he had been promised there would be work available. He could not have made the trip otherwise.

He had been told that there were houses waiting to be built and subway systems. Highways and railroads were planned to connect the cities of both coasts; manpower was needed to turn the blueprints into reality. Wary of strangers, the Italian laborer may not have believed the rosy picture of life in America that had been painted for him. But he was looking for work, and he knew that it was there, waiting for him. When reporters asked a group of embarking immigrants if they were not sad at leaving Italy, their answer was, "Italy for us is who gives us to eat."

Groups of *paesani,* some accompanied by their eldest sons, boarded the boats that left each day, mostly from Naples. As they approached New York some two weeks later, the men were all set to go to work; along with bundles and suitcases, many carried with pride new picks and shovels.

It was at Ellis Island that most of them landed. After 1890, when the federal government began to administer immigration for the entire country, this island off the tip of Manhattan was set aside as port of entry for all steerage immigrants.

In the huge, vaulted reception hall on Ellis Island, thousands of newcomers waited in line for many hours. Greeks, Poles, Russians, Slavs, Armenians, Italians—each was tagged in a different color, according to the language he spoke. For a few anguished moments every man stood alone before the uniformed inspector.

The inspector had two minutes in which to ask thirty-two questions and do a health check. If the immigrant's name was hard to spell, it was rapidly changed to something that sounded more "American." If he had a contagious disease, if he had no funds, or if he was innocent enough to disclose that he had a contract for a job, he was detained on Ellis Island and later shipped back to his home port. If he was healthy and had brought along a little money, (most Italians declared seventeen dollars), he was admitted. Then he could greet his family or friends waiting behind the partition, and they would take the ferry to the Battery, the lowest part of Manhattan island.

Often some enterprising Italian, an earlier arrival to America, would recruit laborers right at the dock. On occa-

Italian family seeking lost baggage at Ellis Island, 1905. Lewis W. Hine, George Eastman House Collection.

Italian worker on the New York Barge Canal. Lewis W. Hine, George Eastman House Collection.

sion, he bribed the immigration inspector.

Following is one young man's introduction to the American dream.

"We were all landed on an island, and the bosses there said that Francesco and I must go back because we had not enough money, but a man named Bartolo came up and told them that we were brothers and he was our uncle and would take care of us. He brought two other men who swore that they knew us in Italy and that Bartolo was our uncle. I had never seen any of them before, but even then Bartolo might be my uncle so I did not say anything.

"The bosses of the island let us go off with Bartolo after he had made the oath. We came to Brooklyn, New York, to a wooden house in Adams Street that was full of Italians from Naples. Bartolo had a room on the third floor and there were fifteen men in the room all boarding with Bartolo. He did the cooking on a stove in the middle of the room and there were beds all around the sides, one bed above another. . . . The next morning early Bartolo told us to go out and pick rags and get bottles."

More often the labor contractor would meet his men at the dock by pre-arrangement and march them off to the railroad station, then to their first job.

In a dramatic autobiography, Pascal d'Angelo describes his trip by train and truck to his first job in the United States. In a forest clearing he found the wooden shack that would be home to him for four years. A kerosene lamp gave off the only light; lumpy beds lined the walls of the room. By an old table sat a man strumming a mandolin. The scene was dismal, yet there was plenty of good, hot soup and fellow townsmen waiting there to greet him.

"And there we all were," d'Angelo writes, "at the beginning of our long years of toil in America. In this country, immigrants of the same town stick together like bees from the same hive and work wherever the foreman or boss finds a job for the gang. And we who had been thrown together almost by chance became like one family."

The job was usually monotonous, but if the boss was kind and the men in good health, they worked with eagerness. Each penny they could save was set aside toward the day when they could go back, or, as more and more of them chose to do, when they could bring the family to join them. They skimped on clothes and food, survived by eating mostly vegetables. When the job was over—the road built, the railroad tracks laid— and the whole group tried to find work together, things could become difficult. Some jobs were far away, and train fare was expensive. On a long train ride, a man with no knowledge of English might lose his baggage or have it stolen. There were jobs where the foreman complained if a man took time to wipe the sweat off his face, jobs where the equipment was old and defective and a man could lose his limbs or his life.

If business was bad (and there were several business re- cessions in the early 1900s), an unskilled laborer from abroad was the first to be laid off. There was no unemploy- ment insurance in those days, no social security. Homesick and broke, many went back to Italy. They were called "birds of passage," these men who worked for a few years and then returned.

Most of them stuck it out, knowing there was no future for them back home. When one job was over, they looked for new work, hoping, as Pascal d'Angelo did, that "somewhere in this vast country an opening existed, that somewhere I would strike the light."

Most laborers found it easier to work for a *padrone,* an Italian boss who brought together a whole group of men, and hired them out as a labor package to an American business firm. There was much criticism of the system; the *padrone* usually collected a fee from both laborers and corporation, and often he would charge outrageous prices for the supplies he sold his men. Some laborers left their *padrone* when they had learned enough of the language and customs to strike out on their own. But there were many who hired out under the same boss again and again, preferring to be exploited by one of their own than by a stranger.

Much of the work was seasonal, temporary; the only security a laborer had was working with familiar people. A man was lucky if he worked in the city, or at least close enough that at night he could go home to Little Italy.

"Little Italy" was the term applied to any neighborhood where Italians settled. There were half a dozen in New York City alone: on Mulberry Street and Bleeker Street, in the Bronx, on Staten Island, on 108th Street and on 9th Avenue. These were the first ones, and many are still there. Later, Little Italys sprang up in all the major cities: in Philadelphia and Chicago, New Haven, Boston, San Francisco.

Fellow townsmen settled in one specific area. When a man sent for his wife, they set up housekeeping near the people from their village. If a man was a bachelor, he moved in as boarder with a family of *paesani*. As soon as possible, he mailed a pre-paid ticket to his special girl, or, if he didn't have one, to a girl from his village who would be a suitable wife. Innumerable girls came to America to marry men they knew only in photographs. At times the wedding was by proxy, in the village church back home. At other times a group of men would go to Ellis Island with a priest to meet the ship that brought their brides-to-be. The priest would perform the wedding ceremony for the entire group in the chapel at Ellis Island.

The women had heard tales of a golden America; their quarters in Little Italy were often a sad disappointment. The area had long been home to immigrants. Old buildings had first been cut up into tenements to house Irish or German families; by the time the Italians came, the tenements were terri-

Italians making neckties in a Division Street tenement in New York City about 1889. Photograph by Jacob A. Riis, The Jacob A. Riis Collection, Museum of the City of New York.

Italian bread peddlers in New York about 1905. Library of Congress.

bly run down. Yet rents were high, and a newly arrived family could not afford much room. A four room apartment might house a large family, plus three or four boarders who helped defray the rent. Five thousand families often lived on the same block.

Despite high rents, ten people to a room, cockroaches and rats, bathrooms shared with many down the hall, it was good to live among one's own. Everyone spoke some form of Italian; the children playing in the street peppered the English learned at school with words of their parents' dialect. On a summer night the women brought their chairs down to the sidewalk to sit and gossip while the children played. The men drank coffee and played cards at the cafe, or in the back room of the grocery store.

Shop signs were in Italian; posters and official notices were printed in two languages. Newsstands carried Italian books and papers; grocers' windows displayed Italian cheeses, sheaves of spaghetti, pink Italian hams, and whole salamis. Pushcart venders moved slowly through the streets, hawking their wares: silvery fish, vegetables from nearby farms, finely shaved ice ready to be scooped into cups and covered with various flavorings.

Feast days were particularly important. The patron saint of the Italian village had crossed the ocean with his people. Transported to America, the *feste* were continued, and some grew into major holidays, like the feast of San Gennaro of Naples, which is still celebrated each September in New York.

Within the foreign city, with its strange language and foods, its hectic life and its outspoken hostility, the Italians in America formed their urban villages where they could carry on the way of life they had known across the sea. For many years they paid little attention to the customs of the land they had chosen. On many issues their attitudes clashed with those of native citizens.

Pietro, an Italian boy, learning to write.
Photograph by Jacob A. Riis, The Jacob A. Riis Collection,
Museum of the City of New York.

They felt, at first, that school was a luxury they could ill afford, and they resented American laws that made attendance mandatory. The children were happy to comply with their family's wishes; work was more to their liking than were books. Yet there were many youngsters who fought their parents for the right to go to school, and some who tried to teach their elders to read and write.

Another viewpoint, which at first divided the Italians from those around them, was their lack of interest in politics. It was a traditional suspicion of strangers that, in many cases, kept them aloof. At other times, it was the hope of returning to Italy. Most new arrivals did not speak the language. When they needed assistance from somebody who spoke English, they turned to a *paesano* who knew his way around: a local lawyer, or a notary public.

Because they were leery of authority, they often did not turn to the police when there was trouble. In many instances, crimes went unreported, or were resolved without help from the law. Such incidents provided ammunition for those Americans convinced that most Italians were criminals. There was never any basis in fact for this belief; crime statistics prove the very opposite. The exploits of a criminal organization know as the Mafia, plus the activities in the United States of racketeers of Italian descent, combined to give the entire community a reputation it did not deserve.

Another institution that the newly arrived Italians did not find to their liking was the Catholic Church. It was an Irish church; before the days of Irish immigration there had been few Catholics in the United States. Although the religion was the same, the practice of it was different in the two countries. The Italian immigrant, turning to the parish priest for comfort and advice, found himself hindered by different customs and by an unsurmountable language barrier. Even the Latin spoken during Mass seemed alien when pronounced by men of Irish stock.

Eventually the Church took steps to correct the situation. Men studying for the priesthood in this country were sent to Italy to learn the language, and Italian priests were encouraged to come to America. Of the many people sent by Rome to this country, two are remembered to this day.

One was Father Pietro Bandini who, while he was still in Italy, had made studies of the Italian immigrant. To pursue his work, the priest requested Church permission to cross the ocean. Appalled by the conditions in which his people lived in the cities, he spearheaded a move to relocate a group of slum dwellers in the country. In Arkansas, he founded the farm settlement of Tontitown, named after Enrico Tonti, who had explored the Mississippi River in early colonial days.

Troubles beset the colony at Tontitown: cyclones and droughts, harassment from the earlier settlers. Father Bandini stayed with his settlers, taught them scientific farming, and turned to the Department of Agriculture for advice in their experiment. Scholar and agriculturist, he did not hesitate to face a mob with gun in hand when his new church was threatened. After some years the colony did prosper, inspiring other groups of Italian farmers to start their own settlements.

Surely the most beloved and most famous of the men and women sent by the Church was Mother Francesca Cabrini. She arrived in 1889, a thin, frail nun in her late thirties who had been chosen by the Pope to minister to the needs of her countrymen in America. She undertook her mission with six nuns, and started by opening an orphanage for Italian children in New York City. To this she added a church and hospital, sending for more nuns to staff them.

The Missionary Sisters of the Sacred Heart had little money, but wherever they went they found Italians willing to contribute food from their shops, their labor, and whatever pennies they could spare. Later, Mother Cabrini moved on to New Orleans, then California, Denver, Chicago, South America. Wherever Italians toiled, she set up a shelter where they could go for care and comfort. She was particularly concerned with the upbringing of the many children orphaned by industrial and mining accidents, and founded a number of homes for them.

These were her words on starting a new mission in Seattle:

"It is very moving to see men and women of advanced years weep with emotion upon beholding their own first Italian church in the New Land. . . . They are reminded of the old country, so long abandoned, and the ever-dear memories of their childhood—the steeples, the squares, the solemn processions in their native land to which they will never return."

She had come to America to help her countrymen, but she grew to love the promise and the vigor of the new country, and she adopted it as her own. Thirty years after her death, a solemn ceremony proclaimed her Saint Francesca Xavier Cabrini, the first American to be so honored by the Catholic Church.

During the early years in Little Italy almost all the men went off to work each day with pick and shovel, which became known as "pickashov." It was their strong backs which provided their keep as they took over the building of the country from previous immigrant groups.

Gradually Italian laborers entered every branch of the building trades. The entire family worked. Children who went to school held jobs in the afternoon in nearby shops, or they shined shoes, hawked newspapers or delivered packages. The women took in sewing and embroidery, made artificial flowers at home. The pay was low, but each cent was needed to feed the family. Many young girls found employment in the garment industry.

Frugal as they were, they set aside every penny they could spare and banked it with a local shopkeeper. Like most immigrant groups, they formed their own banks and mutual aid societies; they had little trust in American banks.

The dream of most families was to buy a small home, where they could grow vegetables in the garden and where the children could play in the sunshine. Many of the men who worked on railroad gangs realized this dream. They bought small plots of land along the tracks from the railroad company, built a house, and formed a colony of their *paesani* in villages outside the cities. Others formed farm colonies far from urban centers: Genoa in Wisconsin; Vineland, New Jersey; and Asti, California, among many others.

For the most part, Italians did not choose to be pioneer farmers, or to grow a single crop on a large isolated tract of land. By the time they came, at the turn of the century, the frontier was largely a thing of the past. But more important, they preferred to cultivate smaller plots, with a greater variety of crops. Accustomed to struggling with the arid soil of Southern Italy, to tilling every possible inch of terraced land up and down mountains, they demonstrated that all soil can be made to produce. Supplying fruits and vegetables to city dwellers became their specialty; for many Italians, the road to success went from truck farming, to pushcart peddling, to the establishment of a store and then a food chain.

In other families, savings went toward the purchase of a small business, usually in the area where the man had first labored. The barber and the bootblack opened his own shop. Men who had carried bricks became foremen, then contractors. Some of them wound up with large building concerns, or moving businesses.

The more Italians came, the more the need grew for the food products they liked. Many opened shops, became importers of olive oil, wine or cheese, while others manufactured these items in America. A few people borrowed the capital to start a restaurant. At first they catered only to Italians, but over the years Americans began to appreciate the flavor and low cost of Italian foods; there is no town in the United States today without Italian restaurants, or pizza shops.

Page from Joseph Byron's Album, "Little Italy" in Harlem, 1890.
Photograph by Byron, The Byron Collection, Museum of the
City of New York.

None of these steps was taken without sacrifice, but the Italian peasants had never known an easy life. What they did not expect was the hostility they met.

As with earlier immigrants, the Italians were accused of liking the crowded conditions in which they lived; with this handy excuse, a landlord did not have to feel too guilty when he overcharged his tenants. They were said to be ignorant, too violent and ready with a knife, too clannish, not interested in becoming Americans. Newspapers called them "the scum of Europe." Labor unions wanted no part of them, claiming they lowered wages. With an Italian name, it was difficult to get any job but the lowest.

Christ in Concrete, a moving novel of life in Little Italy, describes a building accident that kills the father of the young hero. Paul goes to the police station to inquire about his father's body, and the brutal answer comes,

"Oh yeah—the wop is under the wrappin' paper out in the courtyard!"

An explosive instance of American prejudice against Italians took place in New Orleans.

In 1891, the chief of police was shot. Before he died, he said that his attackers were Italian. Whether or not he recognized the murderers, nobody ever knew. Yet orders were given to round up all Italians in the area; hundreds of people were arrested, nineteen were brought to trial.

The judge acquitted most of the men and decreed that three were to be tried again. Sensing the mood of the community, he remanded all the defendants back to prison for their own protection.

The next morning, a newspaper advertisement called a mass meeting, at which all good citizens of New Orleans were urged to remedy the failure of justice.

"Come prepared for action," the notice read. With clubs and shotguns, screaming "Death to the dagoes!" five thousand rioters stormed into the jail house and killed eleven of the nineteen Italians.

Italy broke diplomatic relations with this country, and for once Americans were made to ponder the possible results of their prejudice.

For the most part, American harassment of Italian immigrants took less violent forms. And there were many who appreciated and befriended them. Some Americans tended to romanticize the Italian nature, calling it carefree, high spirited, sunny, hot blooded and dramatic. More realistic observers simply noted:

"These short and sturdy laborers, who swing along the streets with their heavy stride early in the morning and late at night, deserve better of the country. They are doing the work of men."

The work of men gradually started to earn rewards, and by the 1920s many Italians were able to enjoy a measure of prosperity. Meanwhile, the Immigration Act of 1924 drastically cut the number of Italians entering America.

With only a trickle of newcomers, the Italian colonies in this country began to lose some of their characteristics. The older generation might still cling to all their views and habits; their sons and daughters, conscious of the scorn with which Italian things were viewed, strove to Americanize their ways. They did not speak Italian; they adopted American customs in dating; they no longer played "bocce," a bowling game preferred by their fathers, but turned instead to American sports. The entire community took pride in the legendary feats of baseball's Joe di Maggio.

Politically, the Italians became more active, led at the start by Irish politicians who then controlled the cities.

One of the first to become nationally known, and perhaps the most likely to be remembered, was Fiorello La Guardia, born in America of Italian parents. La Guardia was an individualist, and his background is not a mirror of the Italian community. Yet he championed the immigrant at a time when

Fiorello La Guardia. World Wide Photos.

most public servants considered this an unpopular cause.

La Guardia grew up on an army base in Arizona, where his father was bandmaster in the service. As a young man he spent some years in Europe, first in the foreign service and later as a flyer in World War I. Between the consular service and the war he worked as an interpreter on Ellis Island and attended law school at night. As a young lawyer, he helped the garment workers during their first strikes in 1912 and 1913.

All that he learned during these years, the compassion he felt for those oppressed, his quick and eager brain, and his ambition combined to make him a formidable candidate for Congress. The district that he sought to represent was in lower Manhattan; it was peopled by immigrants from all of Europe. La Guardia, a gifted linguist, addressed campaign crowds in Italian, German, Yiddish and Hungarian as well as in English.

He served several terms in Congress, then became perhaps the finest mayor New York City ever had. Plump, tiny, quick-tempered, he delighted his followers with his unorthodox manner. People called him Fiorello, or the English translation, Little Flower. His passion for riding fire engines, fireman's hat on his head, made him a popular subject for cartoonists and photographers. During a long newspaper strike, he read the Sunday comic strips aloud over the radio to the city's children.

These theatrics were only one aspect of the man. He was a true reformer. In Congress he introduced much needed legislation to help the working man, and he was one of the few who fought against discriminatory immigration laws. As mayor, he cleaned up a city riddled with graft. At the end of his life, right after World War II, he was assigned a task that was the culmination of all his years of caring about people. He became head of UNNRA, the relief agency of the United Nations whose task it was to clothe and feed Europe's war-weary people.

Throughout his career, La Guardia was an effective American public servant, and yet he retained a special relationship with the homeland of his parents. For most Italians in the United States, this dual loyalty was troublesome to maintain, and never more so than during the years when Italy was ruled by the Fascist regime.

Recent history shows that Mussolini was a failure, a strutting puppet who led his country to near ruin. Yet during his early years, in the late 1920s and the '30s, the Italian dictator had found favor with many people in this country. Anxious for United States support, Mussolini courted the Italian-Americans.

One young Italian-American expressed his feelings this way:

"Whatever you fellows think of Mussolini, you've got to admit one thing. He has done more to get respect for the Italian people than anybody else. The Italians get a lot more respect now than when I started going to school. And you can thank Mussolini for that."

The respect had been achieved through their own hard work. But whatever the source, the self-confidence of the Italians in America began to increase. As Mussolini's career progressed, the admiration they may have felt for him in the beginning started to fade. When he formed an alliance with Nazi Germany, people in this country began to see Fascism in its true light.

Then came World War II, and Italy was allied with America's enemy. In a nation of minorities it is not rare for one ethnic group to find itself torn between the mother country and the adopted land. It is a time of cruel testing.

The government of the United States showed more compassion for the Italians than it did for other groups; it expressed full confidence in their loyalty, and they in turn proceeded to prove it.

Over half a million sons and grandsons of Italian immigrants fought in the service of the United States, many on Italian soil. In the closing days of the war, many an American serviceman walked up to the door of a farm home in Italy to introduce himself to relatives he had never met.

The post war years have brought startling changes in the life of the Italian communities. Sons and daughters of immigrant Italians are now securely in the middle class, and among the grandchildren there are many teachers, lawyers, doctors and businessmen.

There are still Little Italys, and outwardly, they may appear unchanged. But behind the old facade, apartments now hold all the comforts of an American home. Only the older generation lives there now; the young people have moved to better neighborhoods, or to the suburbs. They come back to a visit, or to buy Italian specialities.

The self-consciousness that once caused some Italians to change their names is a thing of the past; Americans have learned to pronounce Italian names in their own way. Gone, too, is the feeling of suspicion toward those outside the community: Italian-Americans are active in the politics of both parties.

In the cities, we live in what some call the "Italian era." Italian mayors now run countless communities, large and small. There are congressmen, senators, judges and governors who bear Italian names.

A combination of events resulted in raising the image of all things Italian in this country. Americans admired the remarkable comeback Italy made after World War II. Italian movies, fashions and design gained world-wide popularity. As transatlantic travel becomes easy and less expensive, over a million and a half American tourists visit Italy every year. They return eager to practice the language, to enjoy Italian food and wine.

At the same time, Italians continue to be drawn to the United States. Under the revised immigration rules of 1965, newcomers are being admitted to this country at the rate of 20,000 a year per country of origin. Since then, Italians have used every visa number available to them. Many are joining relatives, established here for many decades. Others are skilled young people, eager for new opportunities. Both are finding a ready welcome in the communities where they have settled.

The Jews in
the United States

IN THE SAME MONTH in which Their Majesties issued
the edict that all Jews should be driven out of the Kingdom and its territories—in that same month they gave me the
order to undertake with sufficient men my expedition of discovery to the Indies."

These words, written by Christopher Columbus, are an
apt introduction to the story of the Jews in the United
States.

Columbus' expedition resulted in the discovery of America. In the same year of 1492, the banishment of all Jews from
the kingdom of Spain caused a migration that eventually
brought the first Jewish settlers to America's shores.

Almost two centuries passed between these two events,
years during which the exiled Jews of Spain and Portugal settled in many countries, then moved again, as they had done
since the very beginning of their recorded history.

The Jewish nation as such ceased to exist in the year 67
of the Christian era, when the Romans destroyed the city of

Jerusalem. Even before that time, many Jews had lived in settlements outside their tiny country. What set them apart was their belief, unique in days of old, that there was only one true God.

After the defeat of their country, Jews were permitted to exist as separate religious groups. Some chose to remain in the land of their fathers; the majority left. They traveled east to Persia, south to Ethiopia, west to the lands bordering the Mediterranean, north to the shores of the Black Sea, the Rhineland and as far as England.

Within the various nations they lived as separate communities and enjoyed a certain degree of toleration. For a time, they were involved in all the same pursuits as other men.

Having no civil government of their own, they maintained their identity by obedience to a code of religious law known as the Talmud, which governed every aspect of their lives. Each community had its spiritual leader, the *rabbi* or teacher, who interpreted the sacred law for his people and functioned as judge in their disputes. Yet legally they were subjects of other states, and in those days state and religion were closely allied.

As the new Christianity spread throughout Europe, Jews were looked upon with increasing suspicion. Jewish doctrine did not acknowledge the divinity of Christ; militant Christian rulers were determined to destroy whoever denied the new faith.

After the start of the thirteenth century, constant attempts were made to convert Jews to Christianity. If persuasion failed, force was applied, or else the entire community was banished. Where they were permitted to remain, Jews gradually lost all privileges and rights. Throughout Europe they were prohibited from owning land, joining a guild, or taking part in government. They were encouraged to be traders and money lenders, occupations that brought them scorn and resentment.

Jewish people were hounded from town to town, accused of every crime, blamed for droughts and plagues. In time of stress they were the victims of cruel massacres. Everywhere they were considered inferior and confined to one section of town.

The word "ghetto" was coined in the Republic of Venice to apply to the area that housed the city's Jews. Each country had its own term to indicate the Jewish streets: It was "Juderia" in Spain, "Juiverie" in France, "Judengasse" or "Judenviertel" in the German states, "Jew Street" in England. Whatever the name, the characteristics of the ghetto were similar: gloomy, narrow streets, the houses old and overcrowded. High walls surrounded the area; heavy gates were bolted every night. Jews had to wear special identifying marks on their clothing; if they were found outside the prescribed area they were subject to a fine, or worse.

The sturdy walls of the ghetto offered a welcome measure of protection from hostile mobs. In enforced isolation, Jewish communities grew ever more inbred and self-contained, governed by their own laws and ancient customs. To insure the survival of their cultural and religious heritage they set up schools and synagogues. During peaceful intervals, the pursuit of learning flourished behind ghetto walls and produced outstanding scholars.

In some communities, Hebrew was spoken exclusively; in others, the ancient tongue was combined with the language of the land, creating Yiddish, a blend of Hebrew and German, and Ladino, a variation of Spanish.

In the Spanish peninsula, during the rule of the Moslem Moors, the Jews enjoyed several centuries of peace and well-being, free from most restrictions. In Toledo, Grenada, Cordoba, Seville and other city states, their talent contributed to a civilization rich in art and architecture, philosophy and mathematics, literature and medicine. Later, the Spanish peninsula was unified. New Christian rulers turned on the

Jewish communities, determined to rid the country of all impure influence.

Many Jews converted to Christianity, although some did practice their old religion in secret. Then the Inquisition was established, a secret arm of the Church charged with ferreting out all dissenters. If torture did not make a man repent his heretical beliefs, he was burned alive on a pyre expressly built outside the walls of the city.

Still the Spanish monarchs, the beloved Ferdinand and Isabella, felt their throne threatened by the presence of possible non-believers. In the year 1492, they ordered all Jews expelled from Spain. They also gave Columbus the means to undertake his voyage to the new world.

The Jews exiled from Spain and Portugal fled to various parts of Europe and North Africa; a large number found haven in the Netherlands, which welcomed people of many faiths.

During the century that followed, European powers staked out their claims in the new world; when Dutch settlers sailed to the Caribbean and South America, many Jewish families went with them to help establish Dutch colonies.

From a Dutch settlement in Brazil, the sailing vessel *St. Charles* made its way to the Dutch colony of New Amsterdam in September of 1654. On board were twenty-three settlers of the Jewish faith, at the end of an odyssey that had begun some two hundred years before, when their families fled the Spanish peninsula, migrated to the Netherlands, helped the Dutch colonize sections of Brazil, and were expelled from there by the conquering Portuguese.

Peter Stuyvesant, Dutch governor of New Amsterdam, threw them in jail.

Learning that they were penniless and fearing that "they might become a charge in the coming winter," the Governor wrote home to the Netherlands, seeking permission to expel the new arrivals. He also requested "that the deceitful race—

such hateful enemies and blasphemers of the name of Christ
—be not allowed further to infect and trouble this new
colony."

The Jews of the Netherlands came to the aid of their less
fortunate brothers; influence was brought to bear on Stuyvesant, and the twenty-three newcomers were allowed to stay,
with the understanding that "the poor among them shall not
become a burden to the company or to the community, but be
supported by their own nation."

This was to prove no problem. After centuries of living
apart in Europe, Jews were accustomed to taking care of their
own. Nor did they struggle long. They had been searching for
freedom and opportunity, and in the American colonies they
found both in larger measure than ever before in their history.

Within a year the new settlers were established as merchants, trading in tobacco, fish and furs with other American
colonies, with Indians, and with acquaintances in Europe and
in the Caribbean islands.

During the years that followed, they were joined by other
Sephardic Jews (the name applied to those of Spanish and
Portuguese origin), and founded small communities in the
principal seaport towns: Newport, Philadelphia, Richmond,
Charleston, and Savannah.

The welcome they received in the new world was not
ideal; Puritan-settled colonies would not allow them entry,
and in many cities they had to fight for the right to practice
their religion openly, to trade, to bear arms. Still, most legal
restrictions that bound Jewish life in Europe did not exist in
America.

A few years after the *St. Charles* had landed, New Amsterdam passed to the British and became New York. In 1740,
an act of Parliament authorized citizenship for Protestants,
Quakers and Jews, bringing the Jews closer to complete civic
equality than anywhere in the world.

Not many settlers of the Jewish faith came to the colonies

on the Atlantic seaboard. The need was for skilled farmers, and Jews had for centuries been deprived of contact with the land. The few who did come turned to developing markets, where the products of farms and plantations could be exchanged for manufactured goods.

Accounts of New York life in the 1700s describe the Levy and Lyons Company on Mill Street, with Indians crowding before the warehouse on market day, carrying bales of fur they had brought down the Hudson to the city.

These early settlers of the Jewish faith became well-to-do, respected merchants, proud of their cultural and religious heritage. They built their synagogues and cemeteries, made provisions for the instruction of their young and for assistance to the needy among them. Few though they were, they set up institutions that helped those who came later.

At the outbreak of the Revolutionary War, the Jewish population numbered two to three thousand out of a total of two million people. They gave their wholehearted support to independence for the colonies. For them, the passage, later, of the first amendment to the Constitution, proclaiming religious freedom, was a development of unique importance. Never before had a country been founded where the establishment of a state religion was expressly prohibited.

After 1820, as the United States started to expand westward, there was a rapid increase in the numbers of Jewish immigrants, and a change in the countries from where they came. The first had been of Spanish and Portuguese origin, or Sephardic. In the 19th century, the great majority came from the German states, and from some provinces of the Austrian empire. They were Ashkenazim, northern Jews. The circumstances that moved them to leave their homes were those that also brought America six million citizens of German ancestry. Revolutionary unrest, displacement by industrialization, poverty, and the "America fever" that raged through Central Europe, all these were forces behind the exodus from the Ger-

While I receive, with much satisfaction,
your Address replete with expressions of affection
and esteem; I rejoice in the opportunity of assuring
you, that I shall always retain a grateful remem-
brance of the cordial welcome I experienced in
my visit to Newport, from all classes of Citizens.

The reflection on the days of difficulty and
danger which are past is rendered the more sweet,
from a consciousness that they are succeeded by days
of uncommon prosperity and security. If we have
wisdom to make the best use of the advantages with
which we are now favored, we cannot fail, under the
just administration of a good Government, to become
a great and a happy people.

The Citizens of the United States of America
have a right to applaud themselves for having given
to mankind examples of an enlarged and liberal
policy: a policy worthy of imitation. All possess
alike Liberty of conscience and immunities of
citizenship. It is now no more that toleration is
spoken of, as if it was by the indulgence of one
class of people, that another enjoyed the exercise
of their inherent natural rights. For happily
the

Letter from President George Washington to the
Hebrew Congregation in Newport, Rhode Island,
concerning religious freedom.

man states. And German Jews had an additional motive.

There had been some improvement in the lives of German Jews by the mid-nineteenth century. Some had acquired wealth and social position, and there were among them poets and musicians of renown. A few German states permitted young men of the Jewish faith to attend the university; a group of intellectuals had emerged more concerned with the culture of the outside world and less with holy study.

Yet the majority of German-speaking Jews were still treated as inferiors; they were poor and had remained in the ghetto, whether by necessity or by tradition.

Although there was no active persecution, life in the ghetto was still a straightjacket of humiliating rules. Barred from most occupations, members of the Jewish faith were likely to be small shopkeepers, peddlers, money lenders. They were forbidden to own property, other than the house in which they lived, and had to pay a special tax when traveling beyond their area. In some states, the government even set a limit to the number of marriages that could take place in the ghetto within a year.

It was a time when many Germans were sailing for America; the letters they wrote home stirred the imagination of their countrymen of the Jewish religion.

Between 1820 and 1880, some 250,000 German-speaking Jews came to this country. They crossed the ocean just as the new republic began its westward expansion, and they followed close behind the pioneers.

Most of them had been traders; they had no skill at farming, nor did they have the capital with which to start a business. Jobs that require a knowledge of English were not available to them. Casting about for an occupation, they noted that in rural areas and in recently settled communities, consumer goods were very difficult to get. Farm families had to take long wagon trips into town to purchase the most needed household necessities. The newest immigrants became peddlers.

They used the small amount of money they had brought, or else borrowed enough to buy those items farm families might need. They carried shoe laces for the men, needles, pins, thread and buttons for the ladies, perhaps a bolt of calico and some ribbons, a few knives and inexpensive jewelry. All this went into a pack, which often weighed more than a hundred pounds and was strapped to a man's back.

The peddler set off on foot, and walked from one farm settlement to another, selling his wares. At night he slept in an open field, using his pack as pillow and his coat for a blanket. Sometimes he would be hounded by a watch dog, and other times children would follow after him, jeering. But many isolated settlers came to depend on the peddler not only as a supplier of goods but as a friend who brought them welcome news and gossip.

After he set aside a little money, the peddler bought himself a horse and wagon, widened his territory and added heavier merchandise to his stock. Shoes, pots and pans, copies of the Bible and the New England Primer, axes and little china figurines were among the items he sold to farmers.

There were peddlers who traded among the Indians and gained their confidence at a time when most white men could not. Others followed the gold rush to California; it was in answer to a miner's need for sturdy clothes that a young immigrant named Levi Strauss made the first pair of denim trousers. Almost immediately, they became known as "Levis," as they still are, and earned him a handsome fortune.

As the farm settlements grew, and as the peddler's capital slowly increased, he stopped roving. He opened a little store in a community that appealed to him, and if he had family left in Europe, he sent for them to help him. If he was fortunate and the settlement became a town, his little shop grew with it, at times becoming a department store and an important center in the commercial life of the area.

A few former peddlers, gifted with unusual business tal-

Nineteenth-century immigrant peddler from *Godey's Ladies Book.*

ent, made their fortunes in merchandising. Other peddlers turned to manufacturing particular products that their customers needed, and some of these, too, became wealthy. The great majority succeeded in making a fair living as shop-keepers or small businessmen and were satisfied that their children might have a better opportunity.

Scattered throughout the country, often in areas where there were few other Jews, these newcomers did not stand apart as a solid group. Where there were Germans of other religions, they joined in the same music and athletic clubs. In the larger cities, German Jews formed their own distinctive communities.

The newcomers had little in common with the earlier, settled, Jewish citizens. Between them, there were differences in language, culture, tradition. Moreover, the Sephardims had by then achieved stature and wealth. They were willing to help the German Jews get started in America, but not too anxious to associate with them after that.

Some fifty years after their arrival as immigrants, most German-speaking Jews had become comfortable, middle class Americans, while a handful had achieved true wealth. Few had much education at the start, but they encouraged their sons to go to college and become professional men. They took an active part in the political and cultural life of their cities and created a remarkable number of charitable and fraternal organizations.

Within a few years the capacity of their institutions was tested by an unprecedented influx of Jewish immigrants from still another part of the world. In 1880, the Jewish population in the United States stood at about a quarter of a million. Forty years later, there were two million more. The figures are approximate, since Jews came as citizens of many coun-tries, and no questions are asked in the census about a person's religion.

The new influx came from Eastern Europe, largely from

Russia and from the Polish provinces that were then under her control. Where most previous immigrants had fled from either poverty or persecution, the Jews of Eastern Europe were in escape from both.

The Russian Emperors, or Tsars, held all their subjects in an iron grip. The Jews among them felt the repression most. The great majority were forced to reside in an area known as the Pale of Settlement, and within this region they were restricted to all-Jewish villages. Few occupations were open to them; they were tailors and shoemakers, petty tradesmen or peddlers. Most of them were poor. Their children were forbidden to attend Russian schools, yet the boys were forced to serve in the Tsar's hated army.

Not only was the government anti-Semitic in its policy; the population itself was given to periodic outbursts of persecution known as pogroms, which were carried out with the assistance of the army and the police. Any event could give rise to a pogrom; impoverished and oppressed, Russian masses found release by burning and looting Jewish homes and killing the inhabitants.

In the enforced isolation of their *shtetl*—the Jewish village—Eastern Jews had created a culture almost completely unaffected by Russian life around them. Unlike their brothers in Western Europe and the new world, who by the mid-nineteenth century had begun to respond to the cultures around them, the Jews of Eastern Europe lived in medieval seclusion.

Concern with religion touched each phase of their lives. Their education consisted of studying the holy books, which they pursued with enthusiasm. Even the most ignorant among them knew the test of prayers in Hebrew. The spoken language of the *shtetl* was Yiddish, a German dialect carried east many centuries before. Russian and Hebrew influences had crept into Yiddish, and it had grown into a distinctive language, with a literature of its own.

In each community there were a few who had broken with tradition. Usually they were young men who had been able to attend Russian schools and had gone to live in the cities. With other Russians, they attempted to organize laboring men and bring about some reform in the repressive government of the Tsars.

These two aspects of Eastern Jewish life, the Yiddish culture and the striving for reform, were transfused into American history as a result of the events of 1881.

In that year, Tsar Alexander II was killed by a bomb. An unprecedented wave of riots and cruel massacres swept across the villages of the Pale; a new set of regulations, the May Laws, further restricted the lives of those who remained. Up to that time, the thought of emigrating to America had occurred only to adventurous young men. After 1881, no Jew felt safe in Russia. America became the dream of every family in the *shtetl*, the Promised Land of Bible days.

Seldom did a family have enough money to leave together. The oldest son would go first, or else the father, and as soon as possible send passage money for one more. Those left behind lived in fear that they might not be able to earn a living, that a pogrom would come, or that life in America might prove too arduous for the ones who had gone.

"Schlof Mayn Kind" (Sleep My Child), a song by the Yiddish writer Sholom Aleichem, tells of a women waiting for a letter from America.

Sleep, my child, my sweet, my pretty one,
   Sleep, my darling, sleep.
Sleep, my life, my sweet, my pretty one,
   Sleep, my darling son.

Daddy's gone to America,
   Daddy's gone far away.

Physicians examining a group of Jews at Ellis Island about 1907.
Library of Congress.

> He has left us here a-waiting!
>   Sleep, my darling babe.
>
> In that far-off land, they say,
>   Everyone is blest.
> In that promised land, they say,
>   Weary folk find rest.
>
> Daddy will send us twenty dollars,
>   And his picture too.
> If he's living, sure he'll fetch us,
>   We'll start life anew.
>
> While we wait his happy message,
>   Sleep, my darling, do.
> Sleep, my darling, since you're little,
>   And I watch over you.

The passage money seldom failed to come, not because American streets were paved with gold, but because the immigrants would deprive themselves of all but the barest essentials to bring their relatives and friends out of Russia. For them, there was no looking backward, no yearning for the homeland. They were determined to make this country their permanent home as soon as possible.

By the 1880s the United States had completed the major phase of its expansion. Pioneers were no longer needed; it was a time of industrial growth in the cities. Like the Irish before them, and other groups who came during the same era, Jewish immigrants settled in urban areas, where jobs were available and where they could try to recreate the culture from which they came.

The greatest number settled, at least at first, in New York City. Others chose Chicago, Boston or Philadelphia. They congregated in one area, usually a place vacated by ear-

Immigrants buying and selling wares on Orchard Street on New
York City's Lower East Side in 1898. Photograph by Byron,
The Byron Collection, Museum of the City of New York.

Jewish man ready for the Sabbath Eve in a coal cellar on Ludlow
Street in New York City in the 1890's. Photograph by Jacob A. Riis,
The Jacob A. Riis Collection, Museum of the City of New York.

lier immigrants. In New York City, the Lower East Side was the largest community, the one whose influence has lasted beyond the decades when it was home to over a million Eastern Jews.

It was a short walk from the immigrant depot to the Lower East Side. Abraham Cahan, in his book *The Rise of David Levinsky*, describes the impressions of a newcomer:

"Ten minutes' walk brought me to the heart of the Jewish East Side. The streets swarmed with Yiddish-speaking immigrants. The signboards were in English and Yiddish, some of them in Russian. The scurry and hustle of the people was not merely overwhelmingly greater, both in volume and intensity, than in my native town. It was of another sort. The swing and step of the pedestrians, the voices and manner of the street peddlers, and a hundred and one other things seemed to testify to far more self-confidence and energy, to larger ambitions and wider scopes, than did the appearance of the crowds in my birthplace.

"The great thing was that these people were better dressed than the inhabitants of my town. The poorest-looking man wore a hat (instead of a cap), a stiff collar and a necktie, and the poorest woman wore a hat or a bonnet.

"The appearance of a newly arrived immigrant was still a novel spectacle on the East Side. Many of the passers-by paused to look at me with wistful smiles of curiosity.

" 'There goes a green one!' some of them exclaimed."

The Lower East Side was a world of poverty and hope, of filthy tenements and degrading working conditions, of ancient customs and newly released energy. All the elements of Eastern Jewish culture came together on a few, crowded city blocks. The orthodox beliefs of the old rabbis and pious families lived side by side with the reforming zeal of socialist thinkers. Intellectuals, so long denied the right to speak their minds, published books and newspapers in Yiddish and founded a number of thriving theaters. Everyone was engaged in a fight to defeat the common enemy: poverty.

Hundreds of tiny synagogues were founded in empty lofts and basement rooms where men from the same *shtetl* could worship together and discuss the holy books. Religious schools were started for the children; small classes held in drafty rooms, where unbending rabbis taught Hebrew to restless youngsters.

Along with a concern for preserving tradition went a great eagerness to adopt the new. Free public education was for the Jewish immigrant a priceless gift, one his people had been denied throughout the centuries. Adults and children flung themselves into the process of learning. Evening classes were crowded with men and women struggling to learn English and the concepts of democratic government.

In her autobiography, *Promised Land*, Mary Antin recalls her first day at school.

"Father himself conducted us to school. He would not have delegated that mission to the President of the United States. He had awaited the day with impatience equal to mine. He took long strides in his eagerness, the rest of us running and hopping to keep up.

"At last the four of us stood around the teacher's desk; and my father, in his impossible English, gave us over to her charge, with some broken word of his hopes for us that his swelling heart could no longer contain. . . . I think Miss Nixon guessed what my father's best English could not convey. I think she divined that by the simple act of delivering our school certificates to her he took possession of America."

A high proportion of the newly arrived men were skilled workers who, in Europe, had been employed as tailors, furriers, cobblers, and milliners. Of those without marketable skills, many became street peddlers. On the sidewalks of the Lower East Side—as in so many immigrant communities—everything was sold from pushcarts, to the accompaniment of individual calls to draw the customer's attention. Hats, umbrellas, every possible article of clothing and food were displayed on outdoor stands. Geese and chickens hung by their necks; for 35¢ a pair, a man could buy scholarly-looking eyeglasses and admire his image in a mirror tied to the cart.

Most of the men and many of the women of the Lower East Side found initial employment in the clothing trade, which was developing into a major industry. Of the manufacturers, many were German Jews, glad to employ their newly arrived co-religionists. Often the work was subcontracted to middlemen, to be done elsewhere.

Working at home or in the dismal factories known as sweatshops, men, women and children cut, pressed and sewed hour on endless hour, earning just enough to provide food and shelter. They were paid by the piece, and so they struggled to work faster and faster. Without warning, prices could be cut. Should the worker decide to quit, there was always another greenhorn ready to take over.

The conditions under which they worked would be hard to believe, were it not for the testimony of contemporary writers like Jacob Riis, the crusading reporter who focused attention on slum conditions.

This is how Riis describes a sweatshop in his book *How the Other Half Lives.*

"Up two flights of dark stairs, three, four, with new smells of cabbage, of onions, of frying fish, on every landing, whirring sewing machines behind closed doors betraying what goes on within. . . . Five men and a woman, two young girls, not fifteen, and a boy who says unasked that he is fifteen, and lies in saying it, are at the machines sewing knickerbockers,

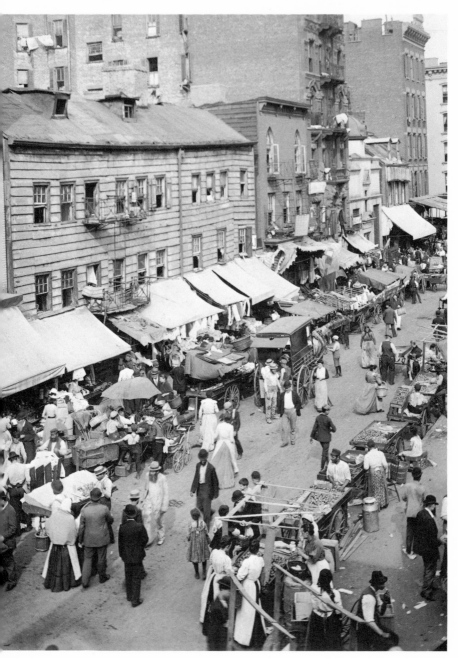
Jewish market. Library of Congress.

'knee pants' in the Ludlow Street dialect. The floor is littered ankle-deep with half-sewn garments. In the alcove, on a couch of many dozens of pants ready for the finisher, a bare-legged baby with pinched face is asleep. A fence of piled-up clothing keeps him from rolling off on the floor. The faces, hands, and arms to the elbows of everyone in the room are black with the color of the cloth on which they are working. The boy and the woman alone look up at our entrance. The girls shoot sidelong glances, but at a warning look . . . they tread their machines more energetically than ever."

The same experience is described in a song, which hints of better days to come.

> Weary days are a tailor's, weary days are his.
> Weary days are a tailor's, weary days are his.
>
> From dawn til dusk he sews away,
> A cent and a song are all his pay.
>
> From dawn till dusk he sits and sews,
> Hunger and pain are all he knows.
>
> From dawn till dusk we work away,
> Time was, we worked a twelve-hour day.
>
> The union broke the twelve-hour day,
> Brought us shorter hours and better pay.

In the development of the clothing industry, the Jewish worker and the social reformer, at times one and the same, found fulfillment for their aspirations. An eight-hour day, the abolition of child labor, a decent rate of payment: These were demands for which the garment workers fought in the early 1900s. The strikes they organized sometimes lasted for months and brought extreme privations to the workers. Many wound up in jail, and some suffered serious injuries. Occasionally men on picket lines were shot and killed. In the end, they created the two great unions of the clothing industry: the International Ladies' Garment Workers' Union and the Amalgamated Clothing Workers of America. When their basic demands were achieved, the unions went on to launch pioneer programs in employee education, insurance, housing and health.

The men who had emerged as leaders of the union movement in the process became influential in the political life of the nation. Meanwhile the Jewish laborer, committed though he was to the improvement of working conditions, prepared himself and his family for an advance in social position.

Regardless of the need at home, most children—especially the boys—were kept in school until they finished high school. If possible, they were encouraged to enter one of the free city universities, after work if not as full time students. As part of the campaign for self-improvement the immigrant and his family took advantage of settlement houses that sprang up throughout ghetto areas.

Many institutions offering aid and counsel had been founded by Jews long settled in this country. To the German-Jewish community, well-established after decades of effort, the arrival of the impoverished, Yiddish-speaking masses was a nightmare. It was in many ways the same reaction the Sephardic community had shown toward the Germans on their arrival. Yet both older groups went to the aid of the newcomers, for reasons both generous and selfish. It was in their own interest, they felt, to Americanize the immigrants as soon as possible. The latter resented their attitude, while at the same time admiring their achievements. Meanwhile all Jews, early settlers and recent immigrants, had to contend with the rise of anti-Semitism in the United States.

Only toward the end of the nineteenth century, as immigration began its rapid rise, did hostile sentiment toward Jews as Jews make itself felt in this country. The first publicized case of anti-Semitism involved a most successful banker, advisor to two American presidents.

Joseph Seligman and his large family were accustomed to spending several weeks a year at the fashionable resort of Saratoga, New York. The Seligmans traveled like other wealthy families of that gilded age; they set out in a private railroad car, accompanied by their maid and valet, a chef, a laundress and several governesses for the children. When they arrived at the Grand Union Hotel in the summer of 1877, they were advised that their presence would no longer be welcome. Hotels, clubs and residential areas announced themselves restricted against Jews. Private schools and colleges admitted Jews on a strict quota system.

The story made headline news the next morning, and was the subject of outraged editorials and sermons for months to come. It was a painful blow to the pride of a family, and an entire group, who had felt secure in American society. Moreover, it marked the beginning of half a century of discrimination against all Jewish citizens.

At first, these instances of antagonism were only of concern to the wealthier members of the community. But as the nineteenth century gave way to the twentieth, all Jews, rich and poor, greenhorns as well as established citizens, found themselves a target for prejudice and bigotry.

The reasons for this development were varied, and some applied to other minorities as well. Recent immigrants who lived in urban areas were blamed, as immigrants had been before them, for the poverty in which they spent their days. Disappointment followed the end of World War I; many people condemned the "foreigners" who had betrayed hopes for a just peace. Some blamed the Pope for all our problems, some the bankers on Wall Street. Others watched the upheavals of the revolution in Russia and were convinced that

Jewish peddler in Chicago.
Lewis W. Hine, George Eastman House Collection.

Jewish grandmother.
Lewis W. Hine, George Eastman
House Collection.

Armenian-Jewish immigrant at
Ellis Island. Lewis W. Hine,
George Eastman House Collection.

Russian anarchists were behind all labor unrest at home.

Jews were an easy target, since there were, among their numbers, many recent immigrants, or "foreigners," a few Wall Street bankers, and a number of labor organizers who were considered "anarchists" by people opposed to all reform. Some Americans began to find it useful to consider all Jews responsible for the downfall of the "real America."

In the 1920's and 30's, it was also fashionable to talk of race, and of the superiority of one over the other. For decades, this theory was accepted by people of integrity, and was used by secret organizations like the Ku Klux Klan for their own ugly purposes.

This agitation resulted in the immigration laws of 1924, which sharply stemmed the flow of new arrivals and in effect put an end to the coming of East European Jews.

Anti-Semitic sentiment reached its peak during the 1920s and '30s, the Depression years, and found a number of influential spokesmen. Henry Ford, founder of the automobile firm, was one of the most outspoken. He used his newspaper, the *Dearborn Independent*, as a springboard for his racist views. In it he reprinted the infamous *Protocols of the Elders of Zion*, a false document supposed to reveal a plot for Jewish world domination. The *Protocols* had been proved a forgery years before Mr. Ford chose to publish them in America. Originally printed in Russia in 1903, the document had been created for the benefit of Russia's rulers, who used it to justify their persecutions.

Before his death, under threat of a lawsuit, Henry Ford apologized to the Jewish community for the slander he spread. For many years Jewish families would not consider buying a Ford car!

By the early 1930s Adolf Hitler had come to power in Germany, and his admirers in the United States were forming organizations such as the Silver Shirts, the Christian Mobilizers, the Christian Front, the Knights of the Camellia, and the

German-American Bund. Shouting and strutting in uniforms and hip boots, these fawning imitators of the Nazi dictator whipped up whatever anti-Semitic feelings they could find among Americans.

These were difficult years for the Jewish community, and their defense organizations were kept busy exposing lies and protecting their members. The Anti-Defamation League and numerous other groups, with the help of Americans of other religious faiths, carried out a campaign against the hate propaganda.

The antagonism, even at its worst, was only part of the picture. Most Americans, and the majority of political leaders, never joined hands with those who spread lies and hate. While bigots were busy with their marches and speeches, Jewish citizens were elected and appointed to positions of trust, to Congress and the governor's chair, to cabinet posts and to the Supreme Court.

To a people who had endured oppression from both government and population for centuries, the United States still offered abundant hope.

Throughout this period, the major effort of the most recent immigrants was directed at earning a decent living, moving out of the ghetto and into a better residential area. The descendents of older families, having achieved positions of responsibility in the professions, often became lawyers and doctors to the newcomers. In Congress, and in the state assemblies, the Eastern European community was usually represented by a member of the older group.

During the 1930s the newest group was busy trying to Americanize. For many families, moving out of the ghetto meant leaving the synagogue, and casting away all signs of Jewish culture. Young men who graduated from high school with names such as Levy or Cohen, applied to college as Leeds and Corwin and, when asked for religious affiliation, replied "none." It was, in part, a response to anti-Semitism. In part it was the urge to conform to the majority's ways, a problem for the children of all immigrants. Had this process continued, it might have signaled the end of the Jewish community as such.

The threat of Nazism to the Jews of Europe made the American community once more aware of its own roots and its responsibilities. In horror, American Jews listened to Hitler's boast that he would end the "Jewish question" once and for all by total extermination. They tried to warn the nation of the tragedy that was in the making. At the same time they gave all manner of help to those few Jews who could escape from Germany and the countries around it.

Had it been easy to find refuge in America, millions of Europeans might have been saved from massacre. But the laws of 1924 were being strictly enforced, and most Congressmen were reluctant to risk a major change. Some 200,000 refugees were allowed to enter, in accordance with the quota system.

So it was that in the late 1930s the Jews of Germany, Austria and Czechoslovakia, reviled by their own countries, mocked and degraded by their fellow citizens, threatened daily with extermination, had to spend endless hours at American consulates waiting for an official to tell them if they would be granted a visa to the United States. The reply was usually "no."

In 1939, the war closed off all avenues of escape. Spreading terror across the face of Europe, the Nazi hordes trapped the Jewish citizens of every country they conquered. More than six million people perished in concentration camps.

The few thousand who had managed to escape from Germany to America before the war, and scattered groups from other European countries, settled in New York and in a few of the larger cities. They were professional and business families, many with university degrees and some knowledge of English. Some had held important posts in Europe before their flight, and in many cases their first jobs in America were

Albert Einstein. *The New York Times*.

menial ones in which their training was wasted.

When the United States entered the war in 1941, the refugees from Europe brought to the national effort a fervor unmatched by most Americans. Anyone who had lived in Europe in the thirties needed no reminder as to why Hitler must be defeated. Young men who had lived here a few short years recrossed the ocean wearing the uniform of the United States. Their familiarity with languages and areas in which the war was fought was invaluable to the armed forces.

War's end revealed the extent of the tragedy that had befallen European Jewry. It was too late to help those who had perished; but there were still huge bodies of homeless men and women wandering about Europe. Allied forces helped large numbers to return home and set up temporary camps for those who had no place to go.

In America, increased pressure was brought to bear on Congress to permit entry to these unfortunate victims. Still afraid to open wide the door, Congress debated for more than three years. Finally a temporary statute was passed, the Displaced Persons Act of 1948, which permitted the entry of some 400,000 people over a period of four years. Of these, about 100,000 were Jewish refugees.

They came from every corner of Europe and bore with them the scars of the tragic experience they had survived. Helping them to adjust, and reflecting upon their tragedy, many Americans became convinced of the necessity for a Jewish nation. Previously, the idea had had little appeal for the Jews in this country. In the aftermath of disaster, most agreed that a homeland had to be founded for those who were not wanted in the country of their birth.

The Jews of the United States were foremost in the effort that created the State of Israel, and many Americans of other religions joined in the work. In 1948, when the United Nations proclaimed the founding of the new country, President Harry S Truman was first in granting it recognition.

Few Americans have chosen to live in Israel, but they have given it strong financial and technical aid, as well as moral and political support.

In the three decades since the end of World War II the Jewish community in this country has undergone great changes. The overriding problem is no longer that of adjusting to a new society; the great majority of Jews are now children and grandchildren of native-born citizens. The American environment has encouraged the development of Jewish talent. In the arts, music and communications, in science and education, medicine, business, the law and politics, Jewish citizens have participated with great vitality. For the most part, their entrance into the wider society does not appear to have caused a decline in their consciousness as Jews. There is a strong commitment to Jewish culture—if not always to the religion—among most of America's five and one-half million Jews.

Today, anti-Semitism has ceased to be an ever-present concern. Jewish organizations, founded for the purpose of combating prejudice, now spend much of their time and resources setting guidelines for other minorities. Judaism is considered one of the major religions; at important government functions a rabbi is present along with ministers and priests.

Yet, even now, once in a while an incident of antagonism toward Jews is noted, either here or abroad. An observer can almost sense a shudder run through the entire community; warnings are issued, ranks are tightly closed. Outwardly secure and successful, full partners in the history of today's United States, American Jews have not quite shaken off the memory of two thousand years of migration and persecution.

From the Orient to
the Golden Gate

NO MAN FINDS IT EASY to leave the land of his birth and start again in different surroundings. If the culture of home is at least similar to that of the new country, adjustment is somewhat less painful.

The European traditions that most immigrants brought had common roots with customs in the United States. Between Americans and the people of Asia, however, the cultural gap was infinitely wider.

The men from China and Japan who landed in California after the middle of the nineteenth century brought with them a different set of religious and social principles, and languages with no resemblance to those spoken here. The shade of their complexion, their clothes and hair style, the shape of their eyes, set them immediately apart. Americans knew little of their ancient traditions; the Chinese and Japanese empires had long lived in isolation from the rest of the world.

In numbers, the immigrants from China and Japan never approached the millions who came from Europe. Yet the hostility they met was such that it caused grave international complications. Their experience in America forms a strange and tragic episode in the history of the great migrations.

It was the cry of "Gold in California!" in 1848 that brought the first wave of Chinese immigrants to *Gum San*, the land they called Mountain of Gold. At first only a few enterprising merchants made the journey, to sell their tea and silks to the settlers and miners in California. Having sold their merchandise, they took to the hills to pan for gold, as did thousands of men of every background who flooded California and became known as the Forty-Niners.

The Chinese merchants wrote home from mining camps to share the news of the discovery. By 1851 there were almost 25,000 Chinese on the West Coast of the United States, most of them at work in the mines. Californians called them "Celestials," since the Chinese Empire was known as the Celestial, or Heavenly, Empire of China.

At first their coming was noted with approval.

"A very large party of Celestials attracted considerable attention yesterday evening," commented the newspaper *Daily Alta California*, in 1852, "while passing down Washington Street, on their way to the southern mines. They numbered about fifty, each one carrying a pole, to which was attached large rolls of matting, mining tools and provisions. . . . They appeared to be in excellent spirits and in great hopes of success, judging from their appearance. They are but the vanguard of a few regiments that are now on their way here from the Celestial Empire."

The Chinese pioneers who came in search of gold were almost all from one small district in southern China, the province of Kwangtung.

To the two major harbors of this area—Canton and Hong

Kong—came the first letters describing the gold strike in California. It was there that young men started dreaming of *Gum San,* the Golden Mountain. Farmers and fishermen went home to their villages after a market day in town and told their families the startling news they had heard on the docks.

In rural China, the word family meant not only wife, husband, and children, but uncles, aunts and cousins, nieces, nephews, parents and grandparents, and ancestors, living or dead. Each member of the family held a well-defined place in relation to every other person. Each had his responsibilities and duties, and could expect his share of affection and respect.

Rules of conduct and morals laid down many hundreds of years before were passed from one generation to another, insuring unchanged traditions. Patience, discipline, respect for learning and wisdom: These were virtues constantly taught and praised. Personal happiness was not the purpose of life, but rather the well-being of the entire group.

Fathers, grandfathers, uncles and cousins, then decided that it would be wise for one of the young men to go in search of gold. Many generations had tilled the same small plot of earth; only for a few months of the year did it produce enough to feed all who depended on it. If the family could acquire more land, everyone's well-being would be insured.

Many families sold what few possessions they had to raise money for the young man's passage; others borrowed. The chosen son, who from earliest childhood had been taught respect for his elders, left for America. He did not go to escape his way of life, but on the contrary, to help preserve it. In the foreign country he planned to live as cheaply as he could; he would save every penny, send it home, and return as soon as possible to end his days a respected, honorable man.

Often the family arranged for the son to marry before he left, in order to help insure his return. The wife, of course, did not accompany him. Her job was to care for children and home, and wait on the older women in her husband's family.

When the men disembarked in San Francisco, they were met by officials of the Chinese Six Companies, the ones who had made the travel arrangements. Calling out in the dialects of the villages represented the company men divided the newcomers into groups according to their native area. Their belongings were piled into a wagon, and the immigrants, in their loose blue cotton shirts and trousers, black hair worn in a long braid at the back, trotted off alongside the cart to the Chinese quarter of the city.

In the mining camps, the Chinese worked and lived by themselves. It would not have occurred to them to join with the other miners, even had they been asked. Accustomed to doing things as a well-organized, disciplined team, they looked upon the Forty-Niners as wild and lawless men, intent only upon their own greed. Before long every mining town had a Chinese section with its own miners, prospectors, cooks and launderers. Special supplies were brought in from San Francisco since the Orientals mistrusted American food.

From the beginning, they set up their own places of worship. In a wooden shack, they would house sacred figures, offerings, candles and incense to be burned before the image of their ancestors. Americans referred to Chinese idols as "joss," a word believed to be derived from the Portuguese "deos," or gods. To the other miners, the Chinese joss house was an object of much curiosity and contempt.

Day after day, the Chinese miners patiently dug and sifted, washing the gravel carefully to work loose tiny particles of the precious metal. A few struck rich finds and promptly shipped the proceeds back to China. Most of them were satisfied to work in areas already picked over by earlier miners, where a man could earn an average of five or six dollars a day, instead of fifty or sixty.

The white miners were an oddly assorted lot. Farmers, clerks, laborers from every region of America and Europe mingled with fugitives from justice, and with ruthless men eager for easy wealth. None of them had much patience with the different-looking strangers in their midst, the Celestials. The Americans scorned the Oriental's religion, ridiculed his clothes and ranted about the way he wore his hair in a braid.

The queue, or pigtail, had been forced upon all Chinese by their own rulers. If a man hoped to return to China, he could not cut off his hair. For white Californians, it became a symbol of all they resented in the "heathen Chinee."

The new, unsettled state of California had little law of any kind to restrain the baser instincts of the miners. As early as 1852, meetings were held condemning the "long-tailed, horned and cloven-footed inhabitants of the infernal regions." From most mining districts the Chinese were gradually driven away, their tents and mining equipment burned. Signs proclaiming "California for Americans," and warnings of "yellow peril" started to appear. A tax on foreign miners was levied, but was never collected from Europeans, only Chinese.

As the 1850s ended, many Chinese were returning home. Of those who stayed, most went into occupations other than mining.

At the start of its statehood, California was a womanless land. Few ladies had accompanied the Forty-Niners on the uncertain and exhausting journey across the land or around Cape Horn; the tasks usually performed by female hands, therefore, went undone, or else were bought at inflated prices.

There was no one to cook, clean, sew, wash or iron for the miners. A man whose shirts were soiled sometimes sent them by boat to Hawaii; they returned months later, washed and ironed at eight dollars a dozen.

The Chinese immigrant, hounded from the mines, saw in this an opportunity for work. At home, he had been a farmer; he knew nothing about washing and ironing. But within a few years there were Chinese laundries all over California, three hundred in San Francisco alone. Later, there was a demand for Chinese laundries throughout the United States.

Chinese miners in California.
California Historical Society, San Francisco.

Chinese washing out gold with a cradle.
California Historical Society, San Francisco.

Chinese restaurants were also started in answer to the need for services performed by women. Miners and pioneers grew tired of cooking their own meals. At first, they were suspicious of the unfamiliar concoctions the Chinese put before them, but they were hungry, and in time grew to like the food.

Other Chinese men found employment as servants, or houseboys. Some settled along the coast and became commercial fishermen. Many went to work as farm hands on plantations that were rapidly springing up; large crews were hired to fill in swamps and marshes and turn them into usable land.

The land of California held enormous resources, but there was little manpower with which to develop them. To the white employer, Chinese workers were a godsend. They worked hard and carefully, seldom complained, accepted meager wages. White laborers, however, resented the competition and brought ever-increasing pressure on the state to keep Orientals out.

Employers continued to request their services. Before long the Chinese Six Companies—each representing one of the six districts of Kwangtung province—were recruiting men not to dig for gold, but to perform whatever tasks where needed, to rent their strength. Coolie labor, these men were called. "Coolie" is probably derived from two Chinese words: *koo*, to hire, or rent, and *lee*, strength.

Coolie labor made its strongest mark in one important area: the building of the transcontinental railway.

A railroad that would join the East and West coasts of the American continent had been a dream of foresighted men for many years. When, in 1850, California became the thirty-first state, pioneers wishing to go there had to face a hazardous overland journey by stagecoach or by ox-drawn wagon, or a voyage by ship down the Atlantic coast, around Cape Horn and up the Pacific.

In 1862, President Lincoln gave the go-ahead to the

construction of a cross-continental line. Two companies were to build the railroad: the Union Pacific, working westward from Nebraska, and the Central Pacific, starting in Sacramento and heading East. Work would be finished when the two lines met.

From the outset, the Central Pacific had trouble recruiting enough men. A dollar a day plus board was not much pay in a state that swarmed with tales of easy fortunes. When Charles Crocker, director of construction work, suggested hiring Chinese immigrants, his superintendents objected. Such small, slight, fragile people could not possibly do the blasting and pickaxing that was needed, they felt. Crocker insisted, and they compromised by sending for fifty Chinese laborers to see how they would do.

Within six months the Chinese Six Companies were importing thousands of men directly from China. Their passage was prepaid and then deducted from their monthly wages of forty dollars.

White workers called them "Crocker's Pets," but they soon found them to be reliable co-workers. Organized into crews, the Chinese coolies lived as a unit, and appointed one of the team to be their spokesman and collect their wages. They brought along their own cooks and tea boys: hot tea, carried in old whiskey barrels suspended from poles, was served the men on the job.

When the line reached the Sierra Nevadas building problems appeared insurmountable. Hundreds of men chiseled away at the mountain, while long human chains pushed wheelbarrows filled with gravel and loose rock. Sometimes the cliffsides had no footholds at all, no ledges on which a man could stand while working. Then Chinese crews wove waist-high baskets with reeds sent in from San Francisco, and had themselves lowered in the basket while they chipped at the rock with hammer and chisel. If the rope did not hold, the basket and the man would drop thousands of feet.

A reporter for the *New York Tribune* described the scene:

"The rugged mountains looked like stupendous anthills. They swarmed with Celestials shoveling, wheeling, carting, drilling, and blasting rock and earth."

On May 10, 1869 the railroad was finally completed. Two locomotives, one from each company, faced each other in Promontory, Utah. Thousands of miles and seven years of work lay behind them. Bands, parades, speeches and ceremonies marked the completion of the transcontinental railroad, and in cities from coast to coast cannons and church bells saluted the event.

Charlie Crocker paid tribute to his workers:

"In the midst of our rejoicing, I wish to call to mind that the early completion of this railroad we have built has been in a great measure due to that poor, destitute class of laborers called the Chinese, to the fidelity and industry they have shown, and the great amount of laborers of this land that have been employed upon this work."

Crocker was convinced, as were most Californians, that the Chinese would go home with their earnings after the railroad was complete. Some did return, but for each of these, two more arrived, still hoping to make their fortune in the land of the Golden Mountain. Some 123,000 landed in the decade after 1870. They arrived at a time when the economy and the political situation in California were both against them.

The financial boom that had drawn thousands to the golden West was over, and most people had failed to make the fortune they expected. A few had gained enormous wealth through investments in the mines; many had lost all they had. There was less need in California for unskilled labor; the railroad was completed, five and a half million acres of swampland had been filled, industries were fully developed. White laborers, newly organized into unions, feared for their future. Their insecurity was taken out on the Chinese.

The anti-Chinese crusade was led by a ruthless agitator named Dennis Kearney. A fiery Irish speaker who addressed countless meetings in vacant lots, Kearney could whip his audiences into a frenzy. He would denounce all who exploited the laboring man: corporations, railroads, and especially the Chinese. Every rally ended with the battle cry, "The Chinese Must Go!". Any Oriental who happened to be passing by during or after the meeting would be kicked, spat on, and often beaten senseless.

The worker's fears of lowered wages were not entirely without grounds; there had been a few instances when Chinese laborers were used as strikebreakers. Kearney's organization, which became the Workingmen's Party, took full advantage of these episodes. He thundered against the "yellow peril," and called upon Americans to "drive every greasy-faced coolie from the land."

Throughout the 1870s there was violence in California and, to a lesser degree, in other Pacific states. Riots, assaults and arson were nightly occurrences in Chinese areas, and inhabitants were advised to keep off the streets after 9 p.m. In 1877, twenty-five Chinese laundries were burned in one night in San Francisco.

"A Chinaman apparently has no rights which a white hoodlum, big or little, is bound to respect," commented one newspaper.

Local and state authorities responded to pressure from the Workingmen's Party by passing a series of regulations affecting every aspect of Chinese life. Public works projects and private corporations were forbidden to hire Chinese workers; local ordinances harassed those who were self-employed. Legislation was passed denying the Chinese their own land; anyone not eligible to become a citizen was not allowed to be a landholder. In the nineteenth century, the law assumed that Orientals were not entitled to citizenship.

Then the pressure on local legislators was transferred to the federal government; the Exclusion Act of 1882 prohibited the entry of Chinese laborers for ten years. This act broke a treaty between the United States and China. Later, the exclusion was extended and made harsher, even forbidding wives from joining their husbands in America.

It was the first time that the American government had singled out the people of one country as undesirable immigrants, and it led to a break in relations with China. For sixty years this infamous statute remained the law of the land.

At no time had the Chinese in this country been as numerous as newcomers from Europe. Even during the decade when Chinese immigration reached its peak—123,000 between 1871 and 1880—four times as many Irishmen were landing and six times as many German-speaking people.

After 1882 most Chinese left this country for good. Against the few who remained, resentment continued. "Not a Chinaman's chance" is a phrase born of this period.

They responded by moving away from the West Coast and by withdrawing further into themselves. At a time when most Americans counseled each other to "Go West, young man," the Chinese hoped to encounter less hostility by moving East.

Wherever they settled, they developed neighborhoods of their own. By the 1900s there were Chinatowns in Texas and Arizona, in Chicago, Detroit, Boston and New York.

The pattern of life in Chinatown was unique. It was a blend of the culture of rural China and a few customs forced on the community by hostile neighbors. The Chinese clung to their traditional clothes, their hair style, mode of worship, language and religion. They had little interest in learning English or in the ways of American politics. They continued

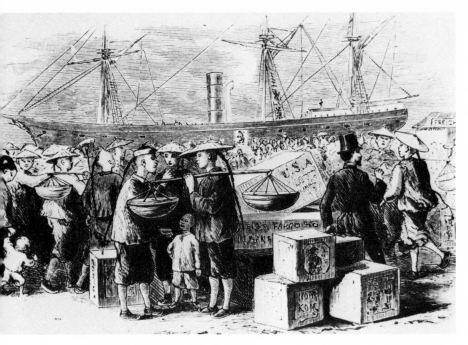

Chinese embarking on ships to come to America.
California Historical Society, San Francisco.

Chinese vegetable peddler in San Francisco.
California Historical Society, San Francisco.

Chinese sidewalk peddler in California, selling toys.
California Historical Society, San Francisco.

Chinese immigrants waiting for a scribe to write letters home
for them. California Historical Society, San Francisco.

to send their earnings home to China so that their families could live in comfort. That they themselves might be considered poor, living in crowded quarters above their place of business, was not important. Status was not measured by what Americans thought, but by the opinion of those at home.

If a man was fortunate enough to have his wife and children with him in the United States—and few were—their life style was that of the village in China. Due respect was given to elders; father's word was law.

Although most parents were themselves illiterate, the children were expected to attend school and be superior students. Evenings they received Chinese language and cultural instruction; in their free time they helped their parents at work. A poor performance in any of these efforts, or misbehavior of any kind, brought dishonor not only on the child, but the entire family.

However, family life in Chinatown was the exception, not the rule. Most men lived as bachelors, even though they might have wives in China. Originally planning only a brief stay in the United States, the immigrant had not brought his wife along. Later if he wanted to stay and send for her, the Exclusion Laws made this impossible. Thousands of men were condemned to lives of loneliness in tiny rooms behind their place of work, cooking and caring for themselves.

Sunday in Chinatown was the only time for relaxation; if a man did not live there, he at least came there to spend his day of rest. He would eat in a restaurant, buy the week's supplies at the grocery store, chat with friends, visit a gambling house. Some sought escape and release by smoking an opium pipe, a custom that enraged and shocked Americans.

There were other aspects of Chinese life that hurt the image of the community. Distrustful of American institutions, the Chinese formed groups that governed and organized their lives. There were family associations, district organizations and tongs. "Tong" means hall or organization. They were first founded as social clubs, and many truly were. But some, especially in San Francisco in the 1880s and '90s, became involved in vice and crime and kept the residents of Chinatown in a state of constant fear.

Newspapers, looking for thrill stories, played up every lurid tale of tong warfare, and editorials condemned all Chinatowns as breeding grounds for vice, crime and dope addiction. Only an occasional perceptive reporter, like Jacob Riis, tried to understand the problems behind the headlines.

"This is a time for very plain speaking on the subject," Riis wrote about Chinatown. "Rather than banish the Chinaman, I would have the door opened wider—for his wife; make it a condition of his coming or staying that he bring his wife with him. Then, at least, he might not be what he now is and remains, a homeless stranger among us."

The overwhelming majority of Chinese had no contact with crime. They spent their lonely days working at occupations that had been predetermined by white America's attitude toward them.

"More than half the Chinese in this country would become citizens if allowed to do so," a Mott Street merchant had remarked in reply to criticism in 1901, "and would be patriotic Americans. But how can they make this country their home as matters are now? They are not allowed to bring wives here from China, and if they marry American wives there is a great outcry. . . . Under the circumstances, how can I call this my home, and how can anyone blame me if I take my money and go back to my village in China?"

No white employer would hire a Chinese; labor unions kept them out; by law they were prohibited to own or lease land. No farmer would hire them as laborers. They had to be self-employed, or employed by one of their own. For fifty years, laundries, restaurants and grocery stores offered a living to a vast percentage of the Chinese in America.

After the turn of the century, time and a series of unrelated events wrought profound changes in the Chinese community.

On April 18, 1906, San Franciscans were awakened at dawn by the hideous roar of an earthquake. In its wake, fires broke out throughout the city, raging for four full days. Five hundred and twenty city blocks were leveled to the ground. Chinatown was destroyed.

San Franciscans hoped that the Chinese would leave the city and resettle somewhere else. The opposite occurred. Many Chinese realized for the first time that home was the Great City of the Golden Mountains, not the ancestral village. The old quarter had been a jumble of overcrowded wooden shacks. The Chinatown that arose after the catastrophe was planned with care and style. Many buildings were patterned on Chinese designs and constructed to fill the needs of the community. A hospital was erected, a housing project, schools and places of worship, both Buddhist and Christian. Gradually it became, and is today, a source of pride to the entire city, and a landmark for every tourist. It has served as a model to Chinese communities in other parts of the country.

During the early decades of the twentieth century, the numbers of Chinese in America decreased constantly, until only 60,000 remained. The older people died, many unmarried men returned to China, and no new immigrants were allowed to enter.

Gradually, much of the violent anti-Chinese feeling spent itself; there were too few to be considered a threat. Besides, California, the cradle of anti-Oriental prejudice, was busy with newer scapegoats.

In time, the federal government began to realize the folly of the Exclusion Acts; a succession of Presidents tried to modify the rules that so insulted the pride of all Chinese. When the United States and China became allied during World War II, President Franklin D. Roosevelt concluded the time was ripe for repeal of the Exclusion Laws.

"Nations, like individuals, make mistakes," he said in a message to Congress. "We must be big enough to acknowledge our mistakes of the past and to correct them."

The bill passed, and the end of World War II saw the arrival of many wives and children from China. The bachelor of Chinatown became a family man, and put down roots. The Communist takeover of mainland China in 1949 further loosened his connections to the old country.

In the past twenty years, the Chinese community has accepted America, and Americans have accepted the Chinese among them. Many no longer live in Chinatown, but even those who do have changed their life style. They have acquired homes and cars, appliances and other possessions they once considered needless luxuries. They have taken every advantage of educational opportunities. Today, there are almost no Chinese among the ranks of unskilled laborers. The younger people have entered fields that command respect and status among Americans; it has proved an effective way of combating whatever prejudice might still remain.

Elements of Chinese culture can still be found, even among the most "Americanized" families. The traditional respect granted to elders has not entirely disappeared; schools with large Chinese-American enrollments find these students among the best-behaved and the most studious. Much has been written about the absence of juvenile delinquency in Chinese neighborhoods; this, also, may be attributed to parental discipline and respect for authority. However, the most recent accounts suggest that even in Chinatown, youthful unrest and ethnic militancy are making themselves felt.

In some parts of the country, Chinatown as a residential area is disappearing. There may still be a few streets with Chinese restaurants, and a few grocery stores, but, at day's end, the owners leave, and drive home to the suburbs.

One tradition draws everybody to Chinatown, even those

whose homes are far away: the festival of the New Year. As far back as 1851 the start of the lunar year was celebrated by the Chinese in this country. Gigantic figures of dragons and lions perform traditional dances on streets thronged with spectators, while musicians beat out stylized rhythms on cymbals, gongs and drums.

In San Francisco and New York, Chinese New Year is popular with visitors of every background. In these cities, Chinatown will always exist. Recent upheavals in Asia, combined with newly liberalized immigration laws, have brought a new wave of Chinese to these two harbor cities, some 70,000 between 1966 and 1970. In New York and San Francisco both, the newcomers have made a dramatic impact on Chinatown. Housing, social services and schools are now inadequate, and there is conflict between established citizens and recent immigrants. Many come from Hong Kong; as modern city dwellers, they differ greatly from the village laborers who landed in the 1800s. Yet they have helped to keep alive the Chinese language and customs, and promise to enrich the Oriental strain in American culture.

Immigration from Japan to the United States started in response to the exclusion of Chinese labor. After 1882, with half the Chinese workers in California sailing for home, and many others leaving for Eastern cities, farm owners and employers found themselves without laborers. It was at that point that they turned to Japan.

Had they needed workers before that time, they would have found no response. Before the middle of the nineteenth century, the Empire of the Rising Sun was sealed off from all contact with the outside world. For more than two hundred years, foreign ships had been banned from Japan's harbors, nor were its citizens permitted to go abroad.

American business interests were most anxious for trade

with the island empire. In 1853, they sponsored an expedition headed by Admiral Matthew Perry. After months of persuasion, he negotiated the first diplomatic and commercial treaty between Japan and a foreign nation.

This started Japan's transformation into a modern country. From a feudal empire it became, in less than fifty years, a fully industrialized nation. The disruption that followed such a radical change led many Japanese to consider leaving home.

During the centuries of its isolation Japan had developed a tightly organized, rigid society that left little room for individual thought or action. Each class had its well defined place in society, from emperor to the lowliest serf. Loyalty to one's class, one's feudal lord, and one's family was expected of every Japanese.

On the volcanic islands which make-up Japan most people made a meager living as farmers. Between shore and mountain, each family laid out its rice paddy and vegetable field in geometric patterns. The family's home was thatched with rice straw; the farmyard held a few chickens, perhaps an ox. Other animals were thought to take up too much room. The farm diet of rice and vegetables was supplemented by fish and sea weed from the near-by coast.

The house was almost bare of furniture, but it always held a shelf for the family gods, some from the Buddhist religion, some from Shinto. Both religions had their place in the home. Running as a thread through life, giving it meaning and unity, were the principles of Confucius, inherited from China so long before that most people were unaware of it.

Not many people were willing to leave this sheltered, well-ordered existence. Less than 1 per cent of all Japanese people emigrated; those who did were driven by the pressures of industrialization and population growth.

The earliest call for Japanese workers came from Hawaii. Ever since the 1820s, American interests had dominated the island kingdom in the Pacific Ocean. Sugar cane and pineapple plantations required large numbers of laborers willing to work hard for very little money. It took three years of constant negotiations before the Japanese government would permit a shipload of workers to seek employment in Hawaii. In 1868, one hundred and fifty-three men were finally cleared; they boarded the ship *Scioto* and prepared to sail away. But at the last moment the government demanded the return of men and passports.

Exasperated, the American consul gave orders for the ship to lift anchor. After months of bargaining, he could not bear one more delay; he kidnapped the men without their government's authorization.

Eventually, Japan's rulers saw the wisdom of allowing people from overcrowded areas to find temporary employment overseas. By then requests were coming in from both Hawaii and California. Between 1891 and 1900, 25,000 people went abroad; in the following ten years, the figure rose to 130,000.

After Hawaii became a territory of the United States in 1900, labor agents from California began to go there to recruit Japanese workers. Enticed by promises of higher wages and greater opportunity, many left the island to try their luck on the mainland.

In Hawaii they had found the work extremely hard but had suffered comparatively little discrimination. People of many different races and countries had been drawn to the islands, and they all lived in relative harmony. On the West Coast of the United States, the Japanese inherited the full weight of hatred that had built up against the Chinese.

A group of Japanese laborers would land in San Francisco and be led from the piers right to the employer who had contracted for their labor. Most of them worked on farms, but there were groups hired by railroad companies, by canneries and lumber camps.

Some individuals wished to live in the city and took jobs

as domestics. The Japanese houseboy was for many decades an institution among California upper class families. For a young man with the proper disposition, this could be good initial employment. It gave him an opportunity to acquaint himself with American life, to learn the language, perhaps to go to school in his free time. By contrast, his compatriots in large labor gangs lived in complete isolation.

On farms, the newcomers were welcomed and praised by landowners eager for help. They picked sugar beets, cantaloups, strawberries, did all the stoop labor nobody cared to do. They worked the fruit orchards, moving across the state as grapes, apples, or apricots were ripe for picking. They were accustomed to farm work, efficient, eager to please, "more docile and obedient than the Chinese," a California newpaper remarked approvingly. Then they began to dream of owning their own farms.

Everywhere they looked, they saw land going to waste. On the basis of their tiny plots back home, an American's front lawn was ample for raising crops. For five or six years Japanese immigrants worked for others, saving every penny that was not needed for their bare existence. Then they made their investment.

They never bought land that was considered desirable by white Americans; it would have been too costly, and besides, it was not available to them. They bought, or leased, property that nobody thought worth cultivating; land that had been broken up by miners, or left a stubble of tree stumps by departed loggers, or delta land along the Sacramento River which had to be drained before it could be planted. It was years before a man could show some profit, but a Japanese farmer was not accustomed to quick results.

Eventually the barren earth turned green, and bore a crop that could be taken to market. Then the old cry of "yellow peril" was heard again. Small farmers feared the competition; plantation owners fretted over losing their labor supply.

"What can we do to protect ourselves," asked the *Pacific Rural Press*, "when thrift, good farming and farsightedness turn out that way?"

The answer was not long in coming. Within a few years these men who had been eagerly recruited were being baited mercilessly.

Agitation against the Japanese began when there were only four hundred in the entire state of California. Mass meetings called for their exclusion, and newspapers accused them of having a low standard of living, of being inferior people, and of being too loyal to the emperor of Japan.

Legislation written to harass the Chinese was put to use against the newest group. For the Japanese, the most punitive was the law denying ownership of land to those ineligible for citizenship. Eventually, they learned to bypass the ruling by leasing property, or by buying it in the name of their children, born in this country.

The crops to which Japanese farmers turned their efforts were those nobody wanted, because the work involved was too backbreaking for people with less patience. They specialized in vegetables like beans, peas and celery, in berries and cut flowers: roses, carnations and crysanthemums. They would acquire land near one another, set up farming communities and cooperatives to market their produce in near-by cities. In time, they came to control certain crops, such as celery, from planting until the customer made his purchase.

If a man had a family, everybody worked in the fields. At harvest time the children hurried home from school to pick the crops. Nobody went indoors until the produce was sorted, crated, stacked, and ready for market.

Most men had come from Japan without a family, and few could afford the journey home to find a wife. A man would write his father asking him to look for a suitable girl. Pictures would be exchanged, a wedding performed by proxy in the ancestral home, and then the bride would leave for California.

The men and women born in Japan, the immigrants them-selves, were known as *Issei,* which means first generation. Their children, born in America, were *Nisei,* second genera-tion.

Before 1908 there were very few *Nisei.* In San Fran-cisco, out of a total school population of 25,000, Japanese students numbered ninety-three. These young people became an international issue.

The ninety-three students were accused of overcrowding the schools and of corrupting the morals of white children. They were older than their classmates, it was said, and there-fore an improper influence. In fact, only two of them were over age, and they were in school to learn the English lan-guage.

In 1906, the Board of Education of San Francisco di-rected all Japanese children to attend a single segregated school. The government of Japan, ever protective of its nation-als abroad, protested the insult. Relations between the coun-tries became tense.

President Theodore Roosevelt summoned the school board and the mayor of San Francisco to the White House, seeking a settlement of the dispute. For Mayor Schmitz, the incident had served as a smokescreen to cover his own corrup-tion. He promptly complied with the President's wishes and withdrew the segregation order. But the President was so alarmed by the bitterness of anti-Oriental feelings on the West Coast that he persuaded the government of Japan to halt the flow of immigrants. The "Gentlemen's Agreement" was a direct result of pressure from a single state.

Indignant, President Roosevelt wrote his son, "The infer-nal fools in California . . . insult the Japanese recklessly, and in the event of war it will be the Nation as a whole that will pay the consequences."

The Gentlemen's Agreement stopped all Japanese labor-ers from coming to America. But the ones who chose to remain

The Big Stick

Cartoon depicting Teddy Roosevelt's decision to keep
Japanese immigrants in public school.
California Historical Society, San Francisco.

Vaccinating Japanese immigrants aboard a Pacific steamship en route to Hawaii in the early 1900's. Library of Congress.

were permitted to send for their families, or for "picture brides," much to the displeasure of Californians.

With the arrival of families, Japanese communities began to take shape in Sacramento, Seattle, Los Angeles, Fresno and in many cities besides the original community in San Francisco. In *Nihonmachi*, the Japanese town, people opened shops and produce markets, rooming houses, restaurants, barber shops, and banks. Nowhere in the white world could an Oriental get a meal, a haircut, a bed; either he supplied his own or did without. House cleaning services and dry cleaning shops became specialties of the Japanese; these were in demand in the outside community. Japanese schools flourished, for most *Issei* parents were determined that their children should learn the language and the ways of the old world. There were special theaters, places of worship both Buddhist and Christian, and innumerable mutual aid organizations. The traditional arts and sports of Japan were taught in storefronts and church meeting rooms.

Rejected by the society around them, the Japanese withdrew to the safety of their own environment. Denied the privilege of citizenship, they took no interest in national affairs. They set no store by American values, but worked toward the day when they could return to Japan. They were not aware that their homeland was changing, that aggressive military forces were gaining power. To homesick eyes, the native village looked as peaceful as ever.

The separateness of the Japanese was used by their opponents to claim that they were unassimilable. Yet Americans would not allow them to belong. Another accusation leveled against them was that their birth rate was too high. They were "breeding like rabbits," it was said; the emperor had ordered Japanese wives in California to have a baby each year. Soon they would outnumber white people! It was true, of course, that many babies were born to the young women who came as picture brides during the first decades of the twentieth century.

Most newly-married people do have babies, regardless of their race. After some years the birth rate dropped off. Meanwhile, the government of Japan was so incensed at the treatment received by its nationals that it stopped issuing passports to young women.

The "Ladies' Agreement" was thus added to the "Gentlemen's Agreement," both steps taken by the Japanese government reluctantly, but of its own accord. Yet even that did not satisfy the hate merchants on the West Coast. In 1924, a section of the Immigration Act barred all Japanese from entering the United States.

The consequence of such open discrimination was far reaching indeed. In Japan, a wave of anti-American sentiment was exploited fully by military interests. In the United States, the legislation drove the immigrants to cling more fiercely to everything Japanese.

Their children would, in time, have bridged the gap, since they were born here and many of their preferences and customs were more American than Japanese. The *Nisei* who were old enough to exert some influence, began to do so in 1930. They organized the Japanese-American Citizens League, their first attempt at making contact with the outside community. The league fought discrimination, encouraged its members to take part in American politics, advised them on matters of career and education.

But the great majority of *Nisei* were still children in the 1930s. Before they came fully of age, World War II had engulfed the United States, and the Japanese community was struck by tragedy.

In 1941, the United States was accustomed to talk of war. The forces of Nazi Germany were sweeping across Europe, and America was lending moral and material aid to England, which alone was fighting against the Axis powers.

In Asia, too, the situation was bleak. A militant Japan threatened neighboring nations. Yet the focus of American concern was Europe, and people argued endlessly over whether or when we should enter the war against the Nazis.

When war did come, it was Japan who brought it about with its attack on our naval base in Hawaii.

It is difficult to recapture the shock, the horror, the disbelief with which Americans listened to the news on that first Sunday in December of 1941. To most people, the territory of Hawaii was a faraway island connected with pineapples and exotic maidens. Few Americans had ever been there; only a handful were aware that we maintained a naval base called Pearl Harbor, which was considered our outpost in the Pacific.

All through the day the fearful details of the attack were broadcast; American ships had been bombed as they lay at anchor inside the harbor, the men asleep on a peaceful Sunday morning. 2,400 Americans had been killed; six battleships and three destroyers seemed shattered beyond repair; the hospital was filled with wounded servicemen and civilians.

On the next day, when President Franklin D. Roosevelt asked Congress to declare war, the nation stood united behind him, the uncertainty of previous months suddenly fled.

What of the Japanese community in America? They, too, were shocked and saddened. They were also ashamed of their homeland and afraid for the future.

In Hawaii, the immediate tragedy left little time for accusations. There were fires to be extinguished, wounded to be helped, emergency work to be done. Civilians of all ancestries took turns at guarding the coastline, afraid that an invasion would follow the air attack. Despite the tension, and despite occasional hostile incidents, the island spirit of *aloha*, love, won out. Of the 157,000 Hawaiians of Japanese descent, the overwhelming majority were treated as loyal Americans.

On the West Coast, there was no tradition of *aloha*. As news of the bombing of Pearl Harbor came over the air, every member of the Japanese community knew there was trouble ahead.

Within three months 110,000 men, women and children had been forcibly moved from their homes in California, Oregon and Washington, and imprisoned behind barbed wire. Among them, two-thirds were American-born, and therefore citizens of the United States. Such denial of the most basic rights of citizens was without precedent in our history. It is worth noting that other ethnic groups whose homelands were on the enemy side—the Italians and the Germans—received much fairer treatment.

In the early months of the war there was much fear of a Japanese invasion of the American mainland. If there was an attack, people worried that the Japanese would rise to aid their kinsmen.

Wild tales went around—and newspapers irresponsibly played them up—of espionage in Hawaii and on the West Coast. *Issei* gardeners were said to have planted flowers in the shape of arrows pointing to airports and defense plants so that enemy airplanes would more easily find their targets. These rumors were repeatedly investigated and found to be completely false.

Yet in early 1942 the leading voice was that of Lt. Gen. John L. DeWitt, the man in charge of the evacuation.

"A Jap's a Jap," the General stated. "It makes no difference whether he is an American citizen or not . . . They are a dangerous element, whether loyal or not."

The President of the United States, congressional leaders, the mayors of most West Coast cities, newspaper editors, and respected columnists, the attorney general of California (later Chief Justice of the United States), Democrats and Republicans, conservatives and liberals . . . all in effect agreed that Japanese, young and old, aliens and citizens alike, were disloyal and dangerous, and should be removed from coastal areas. The few dissenting voices were lost in the general hysteria.

The evacuation order was posted on street walls, on tree

Relocation center at Amache, Colorado. One of ten barrack-type cities constructed for 110,000 Japanese people who were moved from their homes on the Pacific coast during World War II. Each family was provided with a space 20 x 25 feet. National Archives.

trunks and telephone poles. Evacuees were given a few days in which to dispose of their property and goods; they were only allowed to take what they could carry by themselves. In areas considered strategic people were only granted forty-eight hours in which to get ready for departure.

Terminal Island was a fishing community near Los Angeles which happened to be close to Navy facilities. From a small group of shacks built on piles in the water, Terminal Island had grown into a thriving enterprise. A fleet of tuna fishing boats was based there, and modern canneries had been erected. Five hundred Japanese families made their home on the island.

Even before evacuation orders were made public, preying neighbors were calling on Japanese homes, offering to help out. Harassed and frightened, Japanese families practically gave away cars and possessions and entrusted their property to dishonest people.

It was a typical situation, repeated throughout the communities. Many people lost most of what they had; some lost everything.

"Moving day was the most lamentable and sorrowful day in all our life on the Pacific Coast," wrote an elderly gentleman in his diary. "Our foundation, built by fifty years of hard toil and planning, was swept away by Army's Order. It was Awful Nightmare!"

Afraid of trying to resist the order, Japanese families dutifully lined up with their bundles and suitcases at sites where they had been told to report. They were taken by bus to assembly centers reconverted from race tracks and fair grounds. After some months they were moved again, this time to permanent relocation centers.

There were ten centers located in desert lands in the middle of the United States, far from the coast line and all "strategic spots." The centers consisted of rows of tarpaper barracks, each with four or six rooms, with adjoining buildings housing kitchens, mess halls, toilets, medical and recreational facilities. Each camp held at least 5,000 people. In these makeshift towns—hot, dusty, treeless—110,000 people spent two to three years.

They came as families: men and women along in years, aliens because they were denied citizenship, and their American-born children, mostly of school age. There was much friction between the generations; the forced move had disrupted family traditions. An additional cause of strain was the presence of young people born in America, who had received part of their education in Japan. They were known as *Kibei,* and were resented as sympathizers of the Japanese side.

Even from relocation camps, *Nisei* members of the Japanese-American Citizens League continued to work for better treatment for the entire community. They pressured the government for the right to volunteer in the service, and eventually, they won their point. More than one thousand men behind barbed wire signed up for active duty in the war. They fought as a segregated unit, together with large numbers of volunteers from Hawaii. The 442nd Infantry Combat Team served in Italy and France in some of the fiercest battles of World War II. The *Nisei* fought with no regard for self or safety, as if behavior in battle was the only way to prove their loyalty to America. Their casualties ran higher than any other fighting group; they were one of the most decorated units. Often, when a *Nisei* was killed in battle, his parents were not able to go to Washington for his award; they were still in relocation camps.

Young Japanese-Americans also served in the Pacific zone, and were invaluable as interpreters and decoding experts, advance scouts and secret agents.

By 1944, concern over an invasion of the United States had disappeared. The government announced that loyal *Nisei* could leave the relocation camps and move to any area they chose except the West Coast. 5,000 young people were admitted to various universities. Thousands more took jobs in vital war work, in factories and industry and in the government, where their knowledge of Japanese was essential. Often, they settled where no Japanese had lived before. Some communities were hostile; others, like Chicago, Cleveland and Cincinnati, made them feel welcome. During this period, many *Nisei* discovered a new America; they went to the East and the Midwest as a temporary measure, but, by war's end, they had decided to stay. When the government resolved to close the camps many of the older *Issei* joined their sons and daughters who had settled in new areas.

Those who did return to the West Coast had to begin the long, sad process of building anew.

From start to finish, the evacuation had been an injustice and a failure. It had cost the Japanese community some two hundred million dollars worth of property, only a fraction of which was repaid by the government after the war. Today, most authorities are willing to admit that it was not even a military necessity. It was a measure born of all the years of hostility to Orientals.

There are members of the Japanese community today who consider the evacuation a "helpful catastrophe"; it brought them more fully into American life, they say, and gave them an opportunity to prove their loyalty as Americans. How many hold this theory is difficult to say; few care to discuss the episode. In any case, Japanese-Americans have not wasted time in bitter recrimination. In the years since the end of the war, they have established a record of success for which there is no equal, "even in a country whose patron saint is the Horatio Alger hero," one observer notes.

Those returning to areas where they had previously lived faced many changes. Some were too old for field work, or the land they had once leased was in new hands. Often they had to take up different occupations, perhaps move to the cities. In urban areas, other minority groups were living in formerly

Japanese sections. Returning evacuees studied the situation and decided to change with the times. Those who still owned property became landlords to the new arrivals; if the Japanese had been shopkeepers, they adjusted their merchandise to the needs of other ethnic groups.

In some areas, church groups and fair-play committees were helpful in the readjustment. Where once the Japanese had met nothing but bigotry, at war's end there were at least some people who spoke out in their favor.

In other communities, threats, shootings, vandalism and arson greeted their return. Even veterans of the war met with discrimination.

In 1945, a *Nisei* captain on his way home to Hawaii walked into a barbershop in San Francisco. He wore an army uniform with an empty sleeve where he had lost an arm in battle.

"Who were your ancestors? Chinese?" inquired the proprietor of the shop.

"Japanese," replied the captain.

"Sorry," the barber said. "We don't serve Japs here."

The serviceman was Daniel K. Inouye. Fifteen years later, when Hawaii became the fiftieth state in the Union, he was elected a United States Senator. His brilliant keynote address at the Chicago Democratic Convention of 1968 brought him to the attention of the nation.

Today, Americans of Japanese descent are employed in every field, with an unusually high percentage in the professions. They complete more years of schooling than the average white person. The *Sansei*, the third generation, have maintained the traditional devotion to education; colleges and universities find them able, industrious students.

Japanese style in art, design and furnishings is much admired in the United States. Talented Japanese-Americans have combined elements of both cultures, and their efforts have won wide acceptance.

The concern for equal rights that has preoccupied the nation's conscience in the last few decades has found the Japanese community ready to take advantage of every new opportunity.

Where We Stand Today

IT TAKES A LONG TIME for a nation to recognize its errors, and even longer for it to move to correct them. Forty-one years had to pass before the United States was willing to discard the Immigration Act of 1924.

From the day the law was adopted, there were individuals who denounced its provisions and intent. By favoring people from Northern Europe, they maintained, the law implied that nationals of other countries were less desirable; such bias denied America's ideals.

The dissenters worked hard to make their viewpoint known, but in the 1920s and '30s they were few. Gradually, time strengthened their position. Improved research in the social sciences raised doubts about the theory of racial superiority; World War II exposed the dreadful consequences that could follow such beliefs. Meanwhile, the immigrants against whom such outcry had been raised showed that their response to American citizenship was the same as that of earlier settlers.

By the late 1940s, Americans in many walks of life were engaged in attempting to abolish the national origins quota system. The newer ethnic groups joined with religious and civic organizations, newspaper editors, and many congressional leaders in urging a change in the method of admitting newcomers. Four Presidents spoke out for their efforts, arguing that the law was arrogant and absurd and caused bitterness in many countries with whom our nation wished friendly relations.

A number of minor steps were taken over the years to amend certain aspects of the law: emergency acts admitting servicemen's wives, and persons made homeless by war. A few hundred people of Asian descent were permitted to enter. Still, until the 1960s, nothing was done to correct the basic injustice: the discriminatory method of selection.

It remained for President Kennedy to bring before the Congress legislation that would boldly revise the entire procedure. That was in July of 1963, almost four decades after the passage of the initial statute.

John F. Kennedy's interest in the cause of the immigrant was intense and far-reaching. Himself a member of a once-despised minority group, great-grandson of an immigrant cooper, he had been Senator from Massachussetts, a state with a high percentage of nationality groups. He had studied the issue and written widely to urge reform.

He never saw his suggested legislation become the law of the land. Two months after his message to Congress, his life was tragically ended. But his successor took up the task of shepherding the bill through Congress. On October 3, 1965, on Ellis Island, in the shadow of the Statue of Liberty, President Lyndon B. Johnson signed into law the Immigration and Nationality Act of 1965, eliminating the national origins system. Henceforth all immigrants would be admitted first come, first served, on the basis of family ties to American citizens, and of their potential contributions to the nation. Where they were born would no longer make a difference.

The new statute, President Johnson said, "repairs a deep and painful flaw in the fabric of American justice, it corrects a cruel and enduring wrong in the conduct of the American nation. It will make us truer to ourselves as a country and as a people. It will strengthen us in a hundred unseen ways."

The number of newcomers has not been greatly altered by the law; unlimited immigration is not possible in today's America. But those allowed to come—120,000 from this continent, 170,000 from the rest of the world—are judged by their worth as human beings, not by the place where they were born.

In the years since the enactment of the new law, long lists of parents, children, brothers and sisters of people living here have been cleared for entry. Thousands of families from Poland, Italy, Greece, Spain, China and other countries whose nationals had been turned aside in the past, have been reunited.

For these people, the new law has been a blessing, and also for others whose skills place them in one of the preferred categories. For some, the act has had unforseen, and less desirable, consequences.

Men and women with no family ties in America, and others whose occupational talents are not in short supply, are being kept out by the very statute created to repair an injustice. To correct this situation, a number of amendments are being explored by Congress.

Another feature of the new law that has met with criticism is the ceiling placed on immigration from the Western Hemisphere. Before 1965, people of the Americas were permitted to enter the United States without restrictions. In an attempt to be equitable, sponsors of the new legislation set a limit of 120,000. At the time, it seemed a number large enough to satisfy requests.

During the decades when discriminatory quotas were in

effect and few Europeans and Asians were able to enter this country, certain places in our labor market were filled by citizens of the two countries near our borders. From 1925 to 1965, more than 40,000 people a year came from Mexico, and some 25,000 from Canada.

Canadian immigrants, most of them French-speaking, have been crossing the border into New England and the Midwestern states since the middle of the nineteenth century. Almost four million have come over the years, some as temporary workers, but most to settle and take up United States citizenship.

Mexicans go to Texas and California, New Mexico, Arizona, and Colorado. The great majority arrive as farm laborers, frequently moving from one area to another as the crops ripen. Some go home when the year's work is done. Others remain, usually settling in cities close to our southern border, like Los Angeles and San Antonio.

There are five million Mexican-Americans in this country today; some are recent arrivals, others have been American for many generations. Still others trace their roots back to early Spanish explorers. The plight of this ethnic group should be of great concern to the nation. The majority of Mexican-Americans work at underpaid jobs and live in crowded, decaying areas. They suffer from the same poverty and discrimination that greeted earlier immigrant groups. Only recently have they begun to organize in an attempt to secure better treatment for "La Raza," their race, or people.

In the last few years another country close to our border has been the source of newcomers to our shores. Some 40,000 Cubans have left their island each year, coming by plane to Miami. Some are seeking temporary refuge, hoping to return when present policies are changed in Cuba. Others have chosen to remain in the United States. In 1965, when the new immigration law was signed, Cubans were not permitted to leave their island home. Today they are free to do so. The limit of 120,000 immigrants from the Western Hemisphere, which seemed adequate in 1965, may prove to be insufficient and bring hardship to the Cubans as well as others seeking refuge and work in this country. This, too, remains an unsolved problem for those concerned with immigration practices.

Nations undergo constant change. Poverty, discrimination, oppression, no sooner conquered in one part of the world, raise their threatening shadows somewhere else. Many people respond by migrating to a different land, or sometimes to a different section of their own country. The patterns of migration are set by the shifting needs of those who wish to move and by the requirements of the land that receives them.

Today the United States has less need of new people than it did a hundred years ago. The demand for unskilled labor is not great. Our most severe national ills result from our inability to employ that portion of our own population whose training lags behind modern developments. Yet, despite our undeniable problems, people in other countries still look to the United States. The quota of immigrants we are willing to accept is always filled.

Those admitted are, for the most part, carefully chosen. Most of them have a job waiting or a relative to lend them support. A number of private and governmental agencies help them to make the initial adjustment.

Americans who move from one region to another, from Puerto Rico to the mainland, or from the rural South to the big city, have no such guarantees. They reach the cities in large numbers, often without the skills needed in urban areas. They can afford only minimum living space, in quarters already overcrowded. Then the familiar cry is heard that greeted so many millions to our shores: "They'll never learn! They cannot adjust! They'll never be absorbed!"

It is said that social problems today are more complex than they have ever been before. This is true. But we tend to forget how very painful the adjustment was for each new group that made it.

"Perhaps," President John F. Kennedy once wrote, "our brightest hope for the future lies in the lessons of the past."

Epilogue

THE BOY WHO LANDED at Ellis Island in 1907 is today an old man. Most of the people he knew when he first came to America have died. He has been fortunate; in his late years he is still healthy and able to maintain an interest in the world around him.

He has much time for thinking now; he remembers the first few years, when he was so busy earning a living that he had little chance to get acquainted with his new country. Little by little he picked up a few words of English; at night school he added to his education. When he had children of his own, they were encouraged to attend school full time; one of them went to the free university in the city. He has grandchildren now, and two young great-grandchildren; they consider a college education part of their birthright.

He worked until he reached the age of retirement. He never became wealthy, as he had hoped. But he owns a neat house and takes occasional vacations. He reads a great deal, making up for the years when time was short.

He lived through lean times, yet even through the Depression he was able to feed his family. He knows men who were less fortunate; some were thrown out of work and others, unable to get a start in the new country, had to journey back across the sea.

He recalls the prejudice they all met when they first came: the jeers that greeted his strange-looking clothes, and his attempts to pronounce an unfamiliar language. He remembers learning to read the newspaper, only to find, as he made his way from one word to another, that his people were considered inferior, a threat to the American way of life. Older inhabitants urged him to forego his allegiance to his homeland, to drop the old ways, to become rapidly Americanized.

There were many who rushed to conform; they changed their names and moved away from neighborhoods where their friends lived.

Today, the immigrants who were once thought undesirable are held up as examples of virtue and hard work; newer groups are told they are a menace, that they are creating slums and disorder.

The old gentleman, looking back on his years in America, cannot bring himself to join this chorus of contempt. He is puzzled by much of the turmoil of the day. Some of the issues that trouble his grandchildren appear trivial to him. But he remembers his own aspirations, and respects them in others.

If he could meet a group of today's immigrants on their arrival, he would find himself thinking of his own landing, so many years ago.

Today they come by car and plane, or transatlantic liner, and their voyage is comfortable and brief. Many of them have a job waiting or relatives willing to support them until suitable work is available.

Yet, standing in line at airports or on a ship's dock,

waiting for documents to be cleared, the immigrants still wear an anxious look, the fear of an unknown country. Young boys still carry suitcases filled with their favorite possessions, and their dreams of the future in a new land.

Suggestions for Further Reading

Mary Antin, *Promised Land*. Houghton Mifflin (paperback). Biography.

Allan R. Bosworth, *America's Concentration Camps*. Bantam Books (paperback). Non-fiction.

Willa Cather, *My Antonia*. Houghton Mifflin (paperback). Fiction.

Edward Corsi, *In the Shadow of Liberty:* The Chronicle of Ellis Island. Arno Press. Biography.

Ernest Cuneo, *Life With Fiorello*. Macmillan. Biography.

Borghild Dahl, *Stowaway to America*. Dutton. Fiction.

Pietro Di Donato, *Christ in Concrete*. Bobbs-Merrill. Fiction.

Hutchins Hapgood, *The Spirit of the Ghetto:* Studies of the Jewish Quarter of New York. Schoken Books (paperback). Non-fiction.

Elia Kazan, *America, America*. Stein & Day. Fiction.

Fiorello H. LaGuardia, *The Making of an Insurgent*. Peter Smith. Biography.

Jerre Mangione, *Mount Allegro*. Hill & Wang (paperback). Memoirs.

Ernest L. Meyer, *Bucket Boy, a Milwaukee Legend*. Hastings House. Memoirs.

Edwin O'Connor, *The Last Hurrah*. Bantam Books (paperback). Fiction.

Mario Puzo, *The Fortunate Pilgrim*. Atheneum. Fiction.

Jacob Riis, *How the Other Half Lives*. Hill & Wang (paperback). Essays.

Ole Rölvaag, *Giants in the Earth*. Harper & Row (paperback). Fiction.

Leo Rosten, *The Education of Hyman Kaplan*. Harper & Row. Fiction.

Henry Roth, *Call It Sleep*. Avon Books (paperback). Fiction.

Carl Schurz, *Reminiscences of Carl Schurz*. Garrett Press (3 vols.) Autobiography.

John Anthony Scott, *The Ballad of America:* The History of the United States in Song and Story. Grosset and Dunlap. History.

Leonard Wibberly, *The Coming of the Green*. Holt, Rinehart & Winston. Humorous History.

Jade Snow Wong, *Fifth Chinese Daughter*. Harper & Row. Life in Chinese-American Family.

Appendix

IMMIGRATION BY COUNTRY 1820–1968

Country*	Total, 1820–1968	Peak Years
EUROPE		
Austria-Hungary	4,200,000	1880–1920
Denmark	350,000	1880–1900
France	720,000	no true peak
Germany	6,800,000	1850–1890
Great Britain	4,760,000	1860–1890
Greece	540,000	1900–1920
Ireland	4,700,000	1840–1890
Italy	5,100,000	1890–1920
Netherlands	340,000	1880–1920
Norway	850,000	1880–1910
Poland	480,000	1880–1920
Portugal	330,000	1900–1920
Sweden	1,200,000	1870–1910
Switzerland	340,000	1870–1890
U.S.S.R.	3,300,000	1880–1920
ASIA		
China	430,000	1850–1890
Japan	350,000	1890–1920
AMERICA		
Canada	3,900,000	1870–1890, 1910–1930
Mexico	1,500,000	1910–1930, 1950–1965

* This list includes only those countries contributing 250,000 or more immigrants. There are no figures for the years before 1820 as no immigration records were kept then. The figures for Poland between 1899–1919 are included with U.S.S.R., Germany and Austria-Hungary.

Index